Life Lessons from a
Wet Water Walker

by Dan Funkhouser

Life Lessons From a Wet Water Walker
ISBN: 978-0-692-34657-0
Library of Congress Control Number: 2014922803

Copyright © 2014
Published by Dr. Dan and Penny Funkhouser

5715 Vantage Vista Dr.,
Colorado Springs, Co. 80919-5559

http://www.heartbeatint.com

Prepared for publishing by: Orion Productions, LLC.

PO Box 51194
Colorado Springs, CO 80949

www.orion316.tv

Editor: Kelly Johnston

Table of Contents

INTRODUCTION   7

Acknowledgments   11

PROLOGUE   13

CHAPTER 1   17

    THE KINGDOM OF GOD   17

    AMBASSADORS & CITIZENS IN THE KINGDOM OF GOD   19

    THE KINGDOM OF GOD IS AT HAND   22

CHAPTER 2   27

    THE KINGDOM OF GOD
      – DOMINION AND AUTHORITY   27

    FOLLOWING JESUS INTO THE KINGDOM   32

    CONFORMED TO HIS IMAGE   34

    THE KINGDOM OF SELF   37

    JESUS'S COMMISSION TO US   39

CHAPTER 3   43

    POWER IN THE KINGDOM OF GOD:

    THE BAPTISM OF THE HOLY SPIRIT   43

    RESULTS OF THE BAPTISM OF THE HOLY SPIRIT   47

    WALKING IN THE SPIRIT   51

    PURPOSE OF TONGUES   52

    OBJECTIONS TO TONGUES   54

PRAYER TO RECEIVE THE BAPTISM OF THE HOLY SPIRIT 65

NINE GIFTS OF THE SPIRIT   67

FRUIT OF THE SPIRIT   68

PROPHECY, DREAMS, AND VISIONS   69

THE LANGUAGE OF THE KINGDOM OF GOD   69

CHAPTER 4 _____ **71**

WALKING IN THE KINGDOM OF GOD   71

RENEWING OUR MIND   73

MEDITATING THE WORD   74

DIVISION OF SOUL AND SPIRIT   77

PRESSING IN TO KNOW GOD   85

GOD CHANGES US   89

LIVING BY FAITH   93

STEPPING OUT IN FAITH   98

FAITH WALK – NOT FAITH SIT   99

CHAPTER 5 _____ **107**

OUR COMMISSION TO PREACH
   THE KINGDOM OF GOD   107

OBEDIENCE VERSUS REBELLION IN
   THE KINGDOM OF GOD   109

SOWING AND REAPING   110

CHAPTER 6 _____ **119**

GOD'S COVENANT   199

BEING LED BY THE SPIRIT   122

CHAPTER 7 _____ **129**

SPIRITUAL WARFARE   129

CHAPTER 8 _____ **141**

A KINGDOM OF PRIESTS   141

FOUR TYPES OF LOVE   143

A PRIEST LOVES AND DOES NOT JUDGE   146

A PRIEST FORGIVES AND BLESSES   149

JOSEPH'S BETRAYAL – PART OF GOD'S PLAN   154

A PRIEST PRAYS   155

CHAPTER 9   **161**

SPIRIT-FILLED BELIEVERS   161

AS WE FORGIVE, GOD FORGIVES US   163

GOD IS A REWARDER OF OBEDIENCE   165

NEW CREATURE IN CHRIST   167

RESULTS OF BEING BORN AGAIN   169

GROWTH RESULTS   172

MINISTRY OF RECONCILIATION   173

CHAPTER 10   **179**

BLESSINGS OF LIVING IN THE KINGDOM OF GOD   179

THE BEATITUDES   182

KINGDOM OF SERVANTS   188

ANOINTED TO HEAL, DELIVER, CAST OUT DEVILS,
SPEAK WITH NEW TONGUES   192

CHAPTER 11   **199**

THE SUMMATION   199

THE LOSS OF RELATIONSHIP   199

THE PROMISED SAVIOUR   202

ENTRANCE INTO THE PROMISED LIFE   206

THE PROMISED CHURCH   213

THE PROMISED PEOPLE   217

THE PROMISED PROVISION   220

THE PROMISED PURPOSE   222

THE PROMISED FUTURE   223

INTRODUCTION

Pastor Dan Funkhouser and his wife Penny began their walk with Jesus in October of 1973. Since that time, they have been truly amazed and blessed by the opportunities they have had to advance the cause of Jesus in our world. This book, Life Lessons from a Wet Water Walker, is a tribute to what the Lord has taught them about His Kingdom and how every believer can live in the Kingdom and experience all of its glorious riches in the here and now! They want to share the life-giving truth that so many believers today simply have not grasped: God has expressly granted the authority, power, and rights of the Kingdom to each and every believer upon their salvation.

Dan and Penny were born again and baptized in the Holy Spirit in 1973, and three years later were led to start a church called Agape Fellowship in Woodland Park, Colorado. After two years, the church moved a short distance down Ute Pass to Green Mountain Falls. The Lord provided the finances and the church was paid off, and it is still being used mightily of the Lord to reach the lost. Agape Fellowship grew from a small group of nine to well over 800 strong. The church served the congregation and community with a Christian school, Bible College, and a pro-life pregnancy center.

During these early years, Dan and Penny began their formal Bible training. In 1978, Dan graduated from Rhema Bible Training Center. He also went on to earn a Bachelor's Degree and a Master's Degree in Bible Theology from International Bible Institute and Seminary. He holds a conferred Doctor of Divinity degree from the same seminary. Penny graduated from Rhema Bible Training Center in 1981, and later enrolled in the School of Counseling offered at Andrew Wommack's Bible College. She completed that study in the 1990's.

While pastoring Agape Fellowship in the 1980's, Dan began ministering at many crusades and Bible colleges in other countries, primarily in Central and South America. He helped pioneer several new churches, and was voted twice to head the Colorado Springs Ministerial Association. Pastor Dan also had a radio program that aired for many years on KWYD called "The Kingdom Report," where he taught financial freedom based on scriptural principles.

In the 1990's, Dan's focus returned to his family and the pioneering of another church in Colorado Springs. He turned over his ministry in Green Mountain Falls to his staff and began again. During this period, he continued to teach at Bible colleges and served his denomination for five years as the District Superintendent. In 2000, the Lord spoke to Dan and told him to find a successor for the church. He then began mentoring a young man for the position. In June of 2002, Dan turned over the church and began a new adventure.

Today, Dan is the Director of Heartbeat International Ministries, which is an organization dedicated to furthering the Gospel in Cuba and Central and South America through leadership conferences and outreach. Dan and three other men held National Pastors and Leadership Conferences in Central America and Cuba from 2000 until 2005. God supernaturally opened doors, and Dan has ministered from one end of Cuba to the other. He has also had the opportunity to share God's goodness to thousands of believers, despite their government's opposition to Christianity. He still travels to Costa Rica, Nicaragua, Belize and other Latin American countries. Dan has been teaching the Kingdom of God in Pastors' and Leadership Conferences in Central and South America for the past several years. The reception has been phenomenal, and he felt the Lord's leading for him to write this book so the message could be shared with many more believers. It is Pastor Dan and Penny's hope that you will come to a deeper understanding of the Lord, and what it means to be a child of God living in His Kingdom. May God bless you.

Acknowledgements

This book has been the result of several people who are faithful to the Lord and to His service. First and foremost, I would like to thank my loving wife Penny for all of her hard work, and especially for the ability to keep me motivated throughout this project. I would also like to thank my wonderful children, Craig and Christy Decker, for their amazing talents and creative contribution to the cover of this book.

To Kelly Johnston, who has given of her talents as an Editor to faithfully edit this book as her gift to the Lord. To the many partners of Heartbeat Ministries who have helped support this vision and for their prayers for this project. A special thanks to the proof readers who have given of their time and experience to help guide me through this project by their caring concerns for this book.

PROLOGUE

In every life there are moments of decision, revelation or consequence that propel us to the next leg of our journey here on earth. It is our response to these moments that shape us and affect those in our circle—and even have the potential to impact countless others. I can easily reflect on the key events that led to my quest to know the Kingdom of God, and to share it wherever I go.

In October of 1973, my life was completely changed when the revelation of Jesus Christ was birthed into my heart. Like so many, I had gone to church at different times throughout my life without experiencing the reality of the death, burial, and resurrection of Jesus Christ in my heart. This heartfelt revelation—being born again—was the beginning of my relationship with the Lord. After being baptized in the Holy Spirit and speaking with tongues, the language of heaven, my life became consumed with the reality of Jesus Christ. I only wanted to live for Jesus and follow Him; nothing else mattered since then. My desire to live for Jesus soon took on a deeper meaning when in February of 1974, a very unusual young man came to visit me at the Best Western Motel and

Restaurant that we owned with two other partners. He was dressed in a long robe that brought me no little discomfort, and his name was Joseph. He was from Jonesboro, Arkansas, and he ministered to the college kids and to people in the park. We went to our restaurant for lunch, and there he told me the Lord had sent him to give me a scripture, which was Matthew 6:19-34. I had no idea the level of impact this would have on me, but this Word has changed my life and given me confidence to go about the Father's business with great conviction. At the time, I only knew that a very unusual man had said that God told him to give this message to me.

As I began to meditate on the Word in Matthew 6:19-34, the Scripture starting with verse 31 came alive to me: "Therefore take no thought, saying, What shall we eat? or, What shall we drink? or, Wherewithal shall we be clothed? (For after all these things do the Gentiles seek:) for your heavenly Father knoweth that ye have need of all these things. But seek ye first the Kingdom of God, and his righteousness; and all these things shall be added unto you. Take therefore no thought for the morrow: for the morrow shall take thought for the things of itself. Sufficient unto the day is the evil thereof." The very simple fact is that we quote God's Word, but don't respond to it. The Word was saying, "Seek ye first the Kingdom of God." What did that mean? Like many of us, I could spend my life wondering what this means, or I could not pay any attention to it. But, I wanted to know more, since God had brought the Word to me in such an unusual way. I started reading books on the subject and asking people, "What is the Kingdom of God?" One person said that seeking the Kingdom of God first means that you pray to God first and then you go about getting it or doing something to receive it. Well, I wasn't convinced that was it, but I spent about six months praying this way. I would say, "Alright God, I want this," and away I would go to get it myself.

What I found myself praying for was exactly what God had already promised to give: food, clothing and shelter, as well as all things that pertain to life and godliness. This would be like my children praying to God and asking Him to speak to me to make sure that I would feed them today. None of my children ever had to pray and beseech God all day that they might have some food to eat. Nor did they have to do so that they might have a place to live or clothes to wear. That is because I have already committed myself to taking care of them. If they'll just stay within my realm, within our home, within my realm of provision, I will take care of them. Wherever I am, their provision will be. However, if they decide to run away from home and do their own thing, they may starve before I know they have a need. But, when they are in my home, or in my place of provision, I'm committed as a father to give them the best of everything because they are my children.

Likewise, I realized, God wants to take care of our every need in the same way. He will provide our food, clothing and shelter, and He doesn't want us begging for it each day. We are in His Kingdom and, as our King, He wants to meet every need we have. God tells us if we play the game of life by His rules, we win! If we play the game of life by our own ways, we lose. Paul said in Philippians 4:11, "For I have learned, in whatsoever state I am, therewith to be content." God wants us to find that place of contentment in knowing Him because when we learn to trust the Lord, we can put off the cares of this world. We can come into the Kingdom of God as His contented children knowing that He will provide for us while we seek first His Kingdom and His righteousness.

"For what is a man profited, if he shall gain the whole world and lose his own soul?" Matthew 16:26. In short, it was this revelation about the Kingdom of God that has changed my life and given me confidence to go about the Father's business with great conviction. My heavenly Father has graciously taught me so much about His divine provision and the rights he has bestowed on each of us as His heirs and children living in the Kingdom of God. When we grasp the truth of what the Kingdom of God is; where the Kingdom of God is; how you enter into His Kingdom; the blessings in the Kingdom; how you walk in the Kingdom of God; as well as the importance of the Baptism of the Holy Spirit and how it relates to God's purpose for your life, we too can find the contentment the apostle Paul talks about in Philippians 4:11.

CHAPTER 1

THE KINGDOM OF GOD

What is a kingdom? Just the word "kingdom" provokes one's thoughts toward rulership or dominion of a certain place, realm or sphere. And in every Kingdom, there has to be a king. So, just what is the Kingdom of God?

First, we know that God is King in the Kingdom of God. He possesses all knowledge, all power and all control over His vast, eternal kingdom. He sent His Son, Jesus, to be the fullness of the perfect manifestation of the Kingdom here on earth. God was King in Jesus, and because of that the Will of God was done through the life of Jesus. I Corinthians 15:24 says, *"When he shall have delivered up to God, even the Father."* In other words, Jesus had been given this Kingdom as He went about the earth, and in the end He would deliver the Kingdom back up to His Father, God. The Kingdom of God is a true existing kingdom that awaits the child of God. It exists today in the hearts and minds of God's people, and it is ready to be released in our lives as we continue to let Jesus Christ become Lord in our lives. The Kingdom of God is the rule and reign of Jesus in our lives as believers.

Romans 14:17 emphasizes this for us. *"For the Kingdom of God is not meat nor drink,"*—that is, it is not a physical, natural thing—*"but it is righteousness, and peace and joy in the Holy Spirit."* It is righteousness, which is right standing with God which produces in us right doing, living in obedience to the Word—in short, receiving a right relationship with God. It is also peace and joy in the Holy Spirit. Meaning, no matter what is happening in our lives, we can have peace; not worry nor anxiety nor frustration because of who our King is. And we can experience the joy of the Lord in our lives—a true joy, not a forced happiness, but a deep joy in our spirit.

Next, we know that the people of a kingdom can be identified by certain traits, such as language and customs—by their way of life. If righteousness, peace and joy are the key hallmarks of citizenship in the Kingdom of God, what can we learn about achieving these traits and how can we embrace the culture, customs and lifestyle?

Jesus proclaimed the Kingdom of God, and Paul preached the Kingdom of God. So, let's press on to discover the Kingdom. 1 Peter 2 begins to describe God's Kingdom, and will help us identify it, respond to it and be loyal to our King and what He has called us to be. Remember we are to be human beings, not human doings. God has ordained our generation. From the beginning of the earth, even before the foundations, we have been ordained for this generation and for this time for the purposes of God. 1 Peter 2: 9 says, *"But you are a chosen generation, a royal priesthood, a holy nation, a peculiar people; that ye should show forth the praises of Him who hath called you out of darkness into His marvelous light: which in times past were not a people but are now the people of God: which had not obtained mercy, but now have obtained mercy. Dearly beloved, I beseech you"*—I violently urge you—*"as strangers and pilgrims, abstain"*—turn away—*"from freshly lusts, which war against the soul; having your conversation"*—lifestyle—*"honest among the Gentiles: that, whereas they speak against you as evildoers, they may by your good works,"*—not words—*"which they shall behold, glorify God in the day of visitation."* Peter is proclaiming to the church the reality of God's Kingdom. So, what we see is that the culture of the Kingdom of God is a lifestyle of being honest, moral, and dying to the desires of the sinful nature; and proving to all that Jesus is truly alive within us.

AMBASSADORS & CITIZENS IN THE KINGDOM OF GOD

2 Corinthians 5:20 says: *"Now then we are **Ambassadors for Christ**, as though God did beseech you by us: we pray you in Christ's stead, be ye reconciled to God."* God's desire for us is to become His ambassadors. We have been appointed by God to represent His Kingdom on earth. If we study what it means to be an ambassador, we find out that an ambassador does not act as an individual, but as an embodiment of the country he or she represents. God has called each of us to become a walking representative of the Kingdom of heaven here on earth. An ambassador is fully taken care of by his country, so that he may focus on his work. Likewise,

Jesus describes taking care of us in every way—food, clothing, shelter, everything—because we are His ambassadors and He is responsible for all our needs (Matthew 6:19-34). In all ways, He becomes our provider. We are then citizens of heaven, and while we are in the world, we are not part of this world. We are ambassadors of the Kingdom of heaven, and we become that walking representative by living a surrendered life to God's leadership here on earth, allowing the fruits and the gifts of the Spirit to operate in our lives. The fruits of the Spirit listed in Galatians 5:22-23 are love, joy, peace, longsuffering, gentleness, goodness, faith, meekness and temperance. The gifts of the Spirit listed in I Corinthians 12:7-11 are the word of wisdom, word of knowledge, faith, gifts of healing, working of miracles, prophecy, discerning of spirits, divers kinds of tongues and interpretations of tongues.

Our biggest problem with serving God and becoming true citizens of His Kingdom is that we approach Him from our worldly understanding. The United States is a democracy, so therefore the people control the government. In our Constitution we begin by proclaiming "We the people." Our Constitution is the result of people's thoughts and intentions. With our form of government in the United States, we have a Senate, House of Representatives and a President. Their roles are to lead the government based on the will of the people. Anytime the people want to change something, we vote on it and change it. In a democracy, the people can change the law because they created it. The authority is in the people.

We see in Matthew 6:33, *"But seek ye first the kingdom of God, and his righteousness; and all these things shall be added unto you,"* that God's original plan from the very beginning of this earth was a theocracy. A theocracy is a group of people who are submitted one to another in love as a chosen generation, as a royal priesthood, as a holy nation who are pursuing the Lordship of Jesus Christ.

God is the King of His Kingdom, and the Bible is His covenant with mankind. In a kingdom the King's word becomes law. In a kingdom, the people cannot change the covenant, since they do not possess the authority. Only the King can change the law because he created it. That is why in our Bible, God says, *"I am the Lord, I change not"* Malachi 3:6. He is the creator of the covenant, and He does not change. Many approach the Bible from our nation's point of democracy. We want to change what God is saying about certain things, and we try to become God by interjecting our thoughts, ways, wills and contemporary societal standards into the Bible. This is why we have so many translations of the Bible; because man doesn't want to do things God's way, and so he creates a new translation to serve his needs. At the end of the book of Revelation, God has a warning for this kind of action. Revelation 22:19 states, *"And if any man shall take away from the words of the book of this prophecy, God shall take away his part out of the book of life, and out of the holy city, and from the things which are written in."* God does not give mankind the right to change His word; He is the Lord!

What then, are the rules? Seek first what? The Kingdom of God! In Matthew 6:34, the extra benefit of following the Lord is revealed, *"Take therefore no thought for the morrow, for the morrow shall take thought for the things of itself. Sufficient*

21

unto this day is the evil thereof." Each day has enough trouble of its own. What then, is God saying? He is telling us, because we are seeking Him, we don't worry about tomorrow! We don't have to lay awake at night thinking, "Oh, dear Lord, will I have something to eat tomorrow, will I have a place to live or something to wear?" God is telling us, we don't have to worry about these things. If we seek His Kingdom, He will take care of all these things. We are not to worry about things! Why? Because we are His ambassadors! He takes care of us. We are to "cast our cares upon Him." When we begin to understand God's faithfulness to His Word, we will begin to live in victory.

THE KINGDOM OF GOD IS AT HAND

In Matthew 3:2, John came preaching, *"Repent ye for the Kingdom of God is at hand."* "Repent" means an about face or going in the opposite direction. It means you must turn from sin and be born again before you can spiritually see the Kingdom of God. We see Jesus' example in Matthew 4:17-25 when He was coming out of the wilderness and calling men to follow Him. Verse 17 says, *"From that time, Jesus began to preach and to say 'repent', for the Kingdom of heaven is at hand."* The Kingdom of heaven is used in Matthew thirty-two times, and is written to the Jews. To the Jews, it was blasphemy to say the name of God, so Jesus preached the Kingdom of heaven. The Kingdom of God and the Kingdom of heaven are identical. It is not found in any other Gospel. Matthew 4:18-19 continues, *"And Jesus, walking by the sea of Galilee,* saw two brothers, Simon, called Peter and Andrew his brother, casting a net into the sea; for they were fishers. And He said unto them, 'Follow Me, and I will make you fishers of men.' And they straightway left their nets, and followed him."

In just four short years of married life, I had worked in the grocery business, managed stores and both of us had become part owners of a Best Western Motel and Restaurant in Arkansas. It was during this time that Penny and I had noticed the emptiness in our lives. So when we went to a Full Gospel Businessmen's Meeting and heard the gospel of the Kingdom preached, we both eagerly accepted Jesus as our Savior. We decided to follow Jesus after learning what the Bible said, and just as Jesus called the disciples to follow him, that was when I left my net (my vocation), to follow Jesus. It was then that I had found true success—by following God, not my own will. This became a revelation to me, and since November of 1973, God's faithfulness to His word has been proven in my life. Matthew 4:21-23 says further, *"But they left their nets and followed Him and going on from thence, He saw two brethren, James, the son of Zebedee, and John his brother, in a ship with Zebedee their father, mending their nets; and he called them. And they immediately left the ship and their father, and followed him. And Jesus went about all Galilee, teaching in their synagogues, and preaching the gospel of the kingdom."* This is the gospel of the Kingdom, that God was King in Jesus. Let us continue in verse 24, *"And healing all manner of sickness and all manner of disease among the people. And his fame went throughout all Syria: and they brought unto him all sick people that were taken with divers diseases and torments, and those which were possessed with devils, and those which were lunatic, and those that had the palsy; and he healed them. And there followed him great multitudes of people from Galilee, and from Decapolis, and from Jerusalem, and from Judea, and from beyond Jordan."* So Jesus came preaching the Kingdom—the gospel of the Kingdom of God. Jesus was the fullness, the perfect manifestation of the Kingdom of God on earth in man. God was KING in Jesus, and we find in 1 Corinthians 4:20, Paul speaking through the inspiration of the Holy Spirit, *"For the Kingdom of God is not in word, but in power."* It is not in our ability to preach great messages, but the Kingdom of God is in power. The word "power" in the Greek is "dunamis," meaning the miraculous; and pointing to the inherent ability of Christ within our lives that impacts others through spiritual infusion.

Remembering the Kingdom of God in Matthew 10:1-7, Jesus ordained His disciples: *"And when he had called unto <u>him</u> his twelve disciples, he gave them power against unclean spirits, to cast them out, and to heal all manner of sickness and all manner of disease."* All manner—that is, every sickness and every disease. Verse 5, *"These twelve Jesus sent forth, and commanded them, saying, Go not into the way of the Gentiles, and into <u>any</u> city of the Samaritans enter ye not:"* Why? God intended for the gospel to be preached first to the nation of Israel. *"But go rather to the lost sheep of the house of Israel. And as ye go, preach, saying, The kingdom of heaven* (or the Kingdom of God) *is at hand."* It is here and now, it is a present reality. Then what? *"Heal the sick, cleanse the lepers, raise the dead, cast out devils: freely ye have received, freely give."* God is telling them to preach the Kingdom of God and to heal the sick. The Kingdom of God is in power: healing the sick, casting out devils, cleansing lepers, raising the dead, and healing all manner of disease. It goes hand in hand because *"Jesus is the same yesterday, today and forever."* The same Spirit that raised Jesus from the dead is in us.

What is the Kingdom of God? In summary, we see that it exists in the hearts and minds of God's people, position, and an existing location in the heavenlies, the realm of God. As Romans 14:17 summarizes, it is a position of right standing with God and peace and joy in the Holy Spirit. As citizens of the Kingdom, we are to have a distinctive lifestyle that reflects the glory of our King. We see further that we are not only citizens of the Kingdom, we are ambassadors for Christ. As such, God supplies our every need so that we may serve Him without worrying about our provision. Lastly, the power of God is available to us through His reigning in our lives and empowering us by His Holy Spirit. He has given us authority over unclean spirits and diseases so that we might fully serve Him as ambassadors for Christ.

There is so much to learn about the Kingdom of God, so let's move on to explore *just how we enter the Kingdom.*

CHAPTER 2

THE KINGDOM OF GOD – DOMINION AND AUTHORITY

Jesus came into this world to restore God's dominion and authority through our lives as believers, so salvation is more than just being saved from going to hell. It's about God's purpose for our lives. God's plan for us in His Kingdom was also to have dominion and authority over this earth. John 3:3-5 tells us how to enter into His Kingdom, and Genesis 1:26 explains that we were created to have dominion and authority over the earth. Jesus said in John 3:3-5 *"Verily, verily, I say unto thee, Except a man be born again, he cannot see the kingdom of God. Nicodemus saith unto him, How can a man be born when he is old? Can he enter the second time into his mother's womb and be born? Jesus answered, Verily verily I say unto thee, Except a man be born of water and of the Spirit, he cannot enter into the kingdom of God."* Entering His Kingdom is simply accepting what Jesus has done for us: His dying on the cross, His resurrection, and that He is alive forevermore, seated next to God on the right hand side of the throne. When we invited Him to be the Lord of our lives, we gave Jesus the reins over our lives to take over and use us for His purpose. The Spirit of God came into our lives when we were born again.

When we look at Genesis 1:26-28, we see that God created man in His image and after His likeness, and His desire was that we would have dominion over things on the earth. That dominion was lost when Adam and Eve fell in the Garden of Eden, and Satan took title of the earth to become the Prince of this world (John 12:31). However, God is still King! He does whatever He wants.

Man is soon reunited with God and His power through the shed blood of Jesus Christ on Calvary. Romans 5:17 says, *"For if by one man's offence death reigned by one; much more they which receive abundance of grace and of the gift of righteousness shall reign in life by one Jesus Christ."* We find that God restores us not through our works, but through Jesus Christ's sacrifice: His life for our lives. God in us produces through the Holy Spirit to do His righteous works through us, so that we don't glory in them. They are a natural by-product of God in us. Our nature is changed. Matthew 16:24 tells us: *"If any man will come after me; let him deny himself and take up his cross and follow me."* He takes our sinful lives and gives us His righteous life. We then have a right relationship with the Father, and are restored to our rightful place. We are sinful from birth because of the actions of Adam and Eve because of the Adamic curse, not because of our actions! We have also been made righteous because of the obedience of Jesus Christ, not because of our actions!

In John 10:10, Jesus states, *"The thief (Satan) comes not, but to steal, and to kill, and to destroy: I am come that they might have life, and that they might have it more abundantly."* In the Greek language the word for life is "Zoë" which means the God-kind of life. Jesus has come to restore us back to the God-kind of life that Adam and Eve had before the fall. We now have a right relationship with God because of what Jesus Christ has done. He gave His life for our lives; He took our lives and gave us His life, so that we would be made righteous and able to walk with God.

We find Jesus praying in John 17:1-3, *"The hour is come; glorify thy Son, that thy Son also may Glorify thee: As thou hast given Him power over all flesh, that He should give eternal life to as many as thou hast given Him. And this is life eternal, that they might know thee the only true God, and Jesus Christ whom thou hast sent."* In verses 18-19 He continues, *"As thou hast sent me into the world, even so have I also sent them into the world. And for their sakes I sanctify myself, that they also might be sanctified through the truth."* He goes on to say in verse 23, *"I in them; and thou in me, that they may be one made perfect in one; and that the world may know that thou hast sent me, and hast loved them, as thou hast loved me."* Jesus is stating that we are called and made righteous for the purposes of God to be made evident, and that the life of Jesus may be made manifest in our mortal bodies. *"For we which live are always delivered unto death for Jesus' sake, that the life also of Jesus might be made manifest in our mortal flesh"* (2 Corinthians 4:11). The fruit of this is the God-kind of love, which motivates us to reach out to others. We become His messengers sharing the reality of His love, acceptance and forgiveness for a hurting world.

In Psalm 8:4-6, He states, *"What is man that thou art mindful of him? And the son of man, that thou visitest him? For thou hast made him a little lower that the angels, and thou hast crowned him with glory and honor. Thou made him to have dominion over the works of thy hands; thou hast put all things under his feet."* God created man to have dominion over the things of earth. He created us to have authority over everything on the earth. In John 12:31-32 Jesus states, *"Now is the judgment of this world; now shall the prince of this world be cast out and I, if I be lifted up from the earth will draw all men unto me."* Through the sacrifice of Jesus, we find dominion being brought back to mankind.

After the resurrection of Jesus, we find Him stating in Matthew 28:18-20, *"All power is given unto me in heaven and in earth. Go ye therefore, and teach all nations, baptizing them in the name of the Father, and of the Son and of the Holy Ghost; teaching them to observe all things whatsoever I have commanded you; and, lo, I am with you always, even unto the end of the world. Amen."* Jesus is saying to us that because He has risen from the grave, mankind, through accepting Him, has regained dominion over the earth.

We have many today that call Him Lord, yet they do not do what He wills. This is also found in the parable of "Building On a Firm Foundation" in Luke 6:46-49. *"And why call me, Lord, Lord, and do not the things which I say? Whosoever cometh to me, and heareth my sayings, and doeth them, I will shew you to whom he is like: He is like a man which built an house, and digged deep, and laid the foundation on a rock, and when the flood arose, the stream beat vehemently upon that house, and could not shake it: for it was founded upon a rock. But he that heareth, and doeth not, like a man that without a foundation built a house upon the earth; against which the stream did beat vehemently, and immediately it fell; and the ruin of that house was great."* Jesus is talking about two types of people: those that <u>say</u> they are Christ's and those that <u>are</u> Christ's! Those who say they are Christ's live according to their own will, their own way, and their own word. Those who are Christ's live according to His will, His way, and His Word! God has given us the Bible so that we may know the will, way, and Word of God. That is why we must meditate on His Word, so we know when the Spirit of God is talking to us. Isaiah 55:9 says, *"His ways are higher than ours,"* and we will not follow His ways if we don't know them.

Jesus has a way of getting the attention of those that He plans to use for His purposes. He got the attention of Saul on the road to Damascus, even though he was set on killing more Christians. Saul, who became the apostle Paul, was knocked off of his horse, and we see in Acts 26:15-18 that he immediately knew the Lord was there. *"And I said, Who art thou, Lord? And he said, "I am Jesus whom thou persecutest. But arise, and stand upon thy feet: for I have appeared unto thee for this purpose, to make thee a minister and a witness both of these things which thou has seen, and of those things in the which I will appear unto thee. Delivering thee from the people, and from the Gentiles, unto whom I now send thee. To open their eyes, and to turn them from darkness to light, and from the power of Satan unto God, that they may receive forgiveness of sins, and inheritance (the blessings of Abraham), among them which are sanctified by faith that is in me."*

How do we enter into the Kingdom of God? It is through salvation! When we invite Jesus to be the Lord of our lives, we are born again by the Spirit of God. It is then that the process of living in His Kingdom begins. His Spirit within us starts to teach us, guide us, comfort us and allow God's rule and reign to be established in our lives. Jesus was the perfect example of walking out the Kingdom of God on this earth, and our heavenly Father sent Him—complete with the humility of humanity—to be our model.

FOLLOWING JESUS INTO THE KINGDOM

Matthew 16:24 says, *"Then said Jesus unto his disciples, If any man will come after me, let him deny himself, and take up his cross, and follow me."* As believers, we are called to live crucified lives. We are to go to the cross for the forgiveness of sins and seek a life of total denial of anything for self through the power of the Holy Spirit. We are to desire to be dead to the flesh and the corrupt ways of the world. We have come to the end of ourselves, and have entered into the rest of God. Hebrews 4:9-11 also describes this rest, *"There remaineth therefore a rest to the people of God. For he that is entered into his rest, he also hath ceased from his own works, as God*

did from his. Let us labour therefore to enter into that rest, lest
any man fall after the same example of unbelief."*

Similarly, Matthew 16:25-26 states, *"For whosoever will
save his life shall lose it: and whosoever will lose his life for my
sake shall find it. For what is a man profited, if he shall gain
the whole world, and lose his own soul? Or what shall a man
give in exchange for his soul?"* Those that have truly found
Christ are willing to die to themselves, or are prepared to be
made willing to die for the Gospel. Jesus has become the only
issue in their lives. They have no ambition for self, but to see
themselves as sons. For they have truly desired to crucify the
flesh with the affections and lusts. They know that Jesus died
to bring us new life through the death of our self-lives, so that
Christ could be our new lives. For them to live is Christ.

In Romans 8:28, we see God's plan. Jesus was the fullness and perfect manifestation of the Kingdom of God on
earth. God was King in Jesus' life. *"And we know that all things
work together for good to them that love God..."* If you love
God, you'll respond like Jesus because His nature is in you.
Our nature becomes more like God's than it is like the devil's
because we've been born again through our acceptance of
Jesus Christ as Lord of our lives. We resemble that life which
lives in us. Let's go on: *"To them that love God, to them who
are called according to His purpose."* Whose purpose? God's,
not ours! All things work together for those who love God
and who are called according to His purpose. We need to
have a singleness of mind or vision about what God is saying.
The apostle Paul states it well in Philippians 3:13-14, *"But
this one thing I do, forgetting those things which are behind,*

and reaching forth unto those things which are before, I press toward the mark for the prize of the high calling of God in Christ Jesus."

We find in Romans 8:29, *"For whom he did foreknow, he also did predestinate to be conformed to the image of his Son."* Predestinate means to determine beforehand. God determined before we were born that you and I would be the vessels He would use in our generation to proclaim the Kingdom of God to the world. God elected us beforehand. Our part in all this is to choose to believe in the Lord Jesus Christ. In Matthew 16:24 Jesus states, *"If any man will come after me, let him deny himself, and take up his cross and follow me."* To deny ourselves is to realize that our lives have been purchased by God so that His purpose will be manifested through us in the earth. The more we die to ourselves, the more He lives through us. God doesn't just supernaturally come into your life and force Himself on you to make you believe His Word. We have a relationship with Him and, as our faith and trust in Him grow, our relationship deepens and we move closer to oneness with Him by the choices we make. We believe in Him, accept Jesus as Lord and Savior, and allow ourselves to be conformed, by the Spirit of God and the Word of God, into His image.

CONFORMED TO HIS IMAGE

As believers, God predestinates us to be conformed to the image of His dear Son. In the Greek language, the word "image" means: representation or to resemble. So we are called to represent or resemble His Son on this earth. Now if Jesus went about doing good, healing all manner of sickness and disease, proclaiming the gospel, being about His Father's business, doing only those things that the Father wanted him to, and, as in 1 John 3:8, *"Destroying the works of the devil,"* and I am to be conformed to His image, what should I be doing? I ought to be a representative and resemblance of Him. We are called ambassadors on this earth for the Kingdom of God. An ambassador is one who is sent to a different land to represent the authority of the land from which he has come. We've been sent to proclaim the wonders of heaven while we are on this earth. God's desire is to bless us according to John 10:10; He wants us to have an abundant life, and this is ours if we love God and are doing His purpose.

God's hope is for us to follow His Son. That is why He gave the disciples power, so they would have power to go about doing His will. Today, many of God's priests are wandering the earth with no revelation of His purpose for them. Faith comes from hearing the Word. If we don't hear, we will not understand our purpose, and we will not have the revelation of Christ's life living in us. Let's see what the Word has to say about this. Colossians 3:1-4 says, *"If ye then be risen with Christ, seek those things which are above, where Christ sitteth on the right hand of God. Set your affection on things above, not on things on the earth. For ye are dead, and your life is hid with Christ in God. When Christ, who is our life, shall appear, then shall ye also appear with him in glory."*

We are called by God, predestinated to be conformed (pressed) into the image and likeness of His Son. Jesus was the full and perfect manifestation of the Kingdom of God on earth—a man within whom God was king. As we see, we are called to repent and turn from our ways in order that we might see the spiritual realm of the Kingdom of God. It is then that we can follow God's call to die to ourselves and be conformed into the likeness of Jesus. Does this sound easy? No, it's not easy to die to the things that our flesh wants or to the old nature that is in us. Penny was teaching one of our daughters about dying to an area in her flesh when she was only about nine years old, and our daughter was exasperated and said, "What am I supposed to do, just lay down on the floor and die?" Sometimes, we feel that it is so hard to figure out how to overcome these things in our flesh, yet, once we determine that we do want to be like Christ and we want to quit doing anything that does not look like what Jesus would do, the Holy Spirit will be there to help us. He gives us the desires of our hearts. We must desire the Kingdom. Galatians 5:19-21 lists different works of the flesh such as: adultery, fornication, hatred, wrath, division, envy, and drunkenness, to name a few. Also, in Ephesians 4:24-32 is a list of other works of the flesh such as: lying, stealing, corrupt communication, bitterness, anger, wrath, evil speaking and so on. God tells us to change our behavior if these things are in our life. When we read and study the Word, the Holy Spirit will convict us about the things that God wants you to remove from our life. Then, we repent of these works of the flesh in our lives, and He helps us to be an overcomer in these areas.

The Kingdom of God is a crucified lifestyle that produces the Fruit of the Spirit, and that is what makes us a peculiar people. Ephesians 4:26 says, *"Be ye angry and sin not,"* our anger is to use against the devil, and not others.

THE KINGDOM OF SELF

Prior to being born again, we spend our lives building our fantasy kingdom of "self." This kingdom is the one we can rule and reign in according to our own will, motives, skills, desires and abilities. In the kingdom of self, the whole world exists only for my purposes and desires. When we are born again, this kingdom must be submitted to the Lord, and we must get off the throne of our life and allow Jesus to become Lord because there can't be two Lords (the Lord Jesus and our self). We must humble ourselves to the Lord Jesus Christ.

Man is comprised of three different areas: the spirit, the soul and the body. With the spirit we know spiritual things, with the soul we know about ourselves, and with the body we know about the things of the world. We will discuss this more in Chapter 4. Man sits on the throne of his soul, which encompasses the mind, will and emotions or feelings. The soul of man is that part that knows us and that is where our years of selfish living have molded our lives, will and desires. John 12:24-26 says, *"Verily, verily, I say unto you, except a corn of wheat fall into the ground and die, it abideth alone: but if it dies, it bringeth forth much fruit. He that loveth his life shall lose it; and he that hateth his life in this world shall keep it unto life eternal. If any man serve me, let him follow me; and where I am, there shall also my servant be: if any man serve me, him will my Father honour."* Jesus is saying to us that if we love our own natural, selfish life and what we desire in the natural realm, we will lose our eternal life. Like Paul in Romans 7:24 we need to understand the wretchedness of our lives and actions of our fleshly desires and actions.

When we are born again, it is then that we become a new creation (2 Corinthians 5:17). We are given the power of the Spirit to help us overcome who we were so that we can become who He is in this world. This doesn't happen overnight, but it can happen over a lifetime of yielding ourselves to the Lord. The difficult part is found when we suddenly realize that God really does want to take the control of our lives away from us! Most of us would rather just go to church and put a little money in occasionally, and remain in control of our lives. When the Lord comes into our hearts, then begins the battle between the kingdom of self and the Kingdom of God.

John 10:10 tells us, *"The thief cometh not, but for to steal, and to kill, and to destroy: I am come that they might have life, and that they might have it more abundantly."* Jesus has come to set us free from the powers of the devil and to bring us into His kingdom where we can find the abundant life He has prepared for us. In the kingdom of self we live in bondage to the world and the things of the world with its natural desires and lusts. We have lived according to our wants and desires; we have fallen under the power of lust and no longer have control over our own lives. Self is in bondage to sin, and is headed towards a life of self-destruction.

It is at this point that Jesus calls us into a life style of forsaking the world and following Him. Jesus has given us power over all the works of the devil in breaking the bondages of sin in our own lives. This is when our soulish self realizes that, for Christ to reign in our life, self must relinquish the throne of our life. When we make the choice to die to ourselves, we will find it very painful, but not for long. God wants us to be free from the lusts and desires of this world that control our lives, and it will only be through allowing Jesus to be Lord of our lives that we find this freedom, and whom the Son sets free is free indeed! The Holy Spirit has the power to deliver us from the kingdom of self to the Kingdom of God. It is at this point that others will begin to notice a change in our lives, and we begin to witness and share our testimony of what God has done. Others will see because a resurrected life cannot be faked for long. This is the time where agape love (the God-kind of love) begins to manifest in our lives, and the things of God become our focus.

JESUS'S COMMISSION TO US

Jesus spoke to the eleven disciples after his resurrection saying in Matthew 28:19, *"All power is given unto me in heaven and in earth. Go ye therefore, and teach all nations, baptizing them in the name of the Father and of the Son and of the Holy Ghost; teaching them to observe all things whatsoever I have*

39

commanded you: and, lo, I am with you always, even unto the end of the world." Then we see what Luke wrote in Acts. (This is the second book written by Luke who was a medical doctor. He wrote the gospel of Luke, which is the story of Jesus, and the book of Acts, also about Jesus working by the Holy Spirit in and through the lives of the new believers.) Acts 1:1 says *"The former treatise have I made, O Theophilus, of all that Jesus began. Both to do and teach, until the day in which he was taken up, after that he through the Holy Ghost had given commandments unto the apostles whom he had chosen: To whom also he showed himself alive after his passion by many infallible proofs, being seen of them forty days, and speaking of the things pertaining to the kingdom of God."*

The last forty days Jesus spoke to His disciples about what He determined to be of great importance! The subject that was near and dear to His heart was the Kingdom of God. In Colossians 1:13 we're told, *"Who hath delivered us from the power of darkness, and hath translated us into the kingdom of his dear Son."* What Kingdom was that? The Kingdom of God! We have been translated out of darkness (that is, ignorance of God and His ways) and into the Kingdom of God. We find the apostle Paul in his last two years ministering in Rome in Acts 28:30, *"And Paul dwelt two whole years in his own hired house, and received all that came in unto him."* He didn't go out and try to evangelize; instead he received all who would come to him. Verse 31 continues, *"Preaching the kingdom of God, and teaching those things which concern the Lord Jesus Christ, with all confidence, no man forbidding him."* The apostle Paul spent these two years preaching the Kingdom of

God—not faith, not love, not tongues, not prosperity, nothing other than the Kingdom of God. Now, all these things I have listed are a *part* of the Kingdom of God, but the important thing is that we understand who is King in our lives!

When we begin to meditate on what God is saying and see it repeated over and over in Scripture, it will begin to sink into our hearts and bring revelation to us. Once we begin to understand the Kingdom of God and allow Him full ownership of our lives, we will understand the purpose for our lives and being translated into the Kingdom of His dear Son. Matthew 11:12 says, *"The kingdom of heaven suffereth violence, and the violent take it by force."* Our anger is to be directed towards the devil. We must become single-minded in our pursuit of God and His Kingdom within us. When we do so, our problems concerning food, clothing and shelter are over. Either it is true or it is a lie. You need to make a decision about what God's Word is saying, and if it rings true to you. If it is true, and we are not living in it, then it is our fault. God has presented it to mankind, and mankind must make the choice. He is willing to lead, guide and direct our lives for His purpose and has agreed to take care of us in return if we yield our lives to Him. After Penny and I became Christians, we both began to study the scriptures so that we could know what Jesus was saying to us. We took the scriptures literally, which began to change our thinking as we renewed our minds to God's ways. We soon realized that God wanted to take care of every need that we had. As young Christians, however, we did not know what that looked like, and the difficult part was in believing that He wanted to do everything for us. But, we stepped forward in faith and turned to God for every area and need of our life. We did pray about food, clothing, shelter, and jobs because at that time we didn't understand God's plan of provision for those who are part of His Kingdom.

In the next chapter, we want to share how another step of faith—the Baptism of the Holy Spirit—changed our lives. Penny had asked the Lord to give her the Baptism of the Holy Spirit after we got home from a Full Gospel Businessmen's Meeting. Although neither of us went forward for salvation at the meeting, we both heard how to get saved there. Penny asked me if I was saved on the ride home, and I began to tell her that I believed that Jesus died for my sins and that He rose from the dead, and was sitting on the right hand side of God. As I shared this with her, I felt the Holy Spirit upon me, so I knew at that time I had received salvation. Penny didn't ask for salvation until hours after that meeting when she couldn't sleep. She asked the Lord to give her what the people at the meeting had received! Upon asking for that, she received salvation and the Baptism of the Holy Spirit. I received the Baptism in a meeting one week later with Bill Basanski, a former teacher at Oral Roberts University. What a wonderful way to start our walk with the Lord Jesus: being empowered to be witnesses, sharing truth with family, friends and employees.

CHAPTER 3

POWER IN THE KINGDOM OF GOD: THE BAPTISM OF THE HOLY SPIRIT

We have learned that the Kingdom of God is not some faraway place or final destination. It is here today in the hearts and minds of God's people—it exists as a position of right standing with God rather than a physical location in this earth. However, it is the realm of God and the place of his existence in the heavenlies. We enter into the Kingdom through salvation, that is, by asking Jesus to be Lord of our lives. Once we are citizens of the Kingdom, God has promised to provide for our every need as we follow Jesus' example and serve God as His ambassadors. God has even promised to provide us with His power so that we are able to serve Him in a complete, whole and abundant manner!

The power of God that is available to us through the Kingdom of God is called the Baptism of the Holy Spirit. This power is promised to every believer, and it is so important and vital to every believer's success in living a Spirit-filled life that I have provided a more in-depth study about it in this chapter.

Penny and I received the Baptism of the Holy Spirit in 1973 and our life took a drastic change. All of a sudden, we had been empowered by the Spirit of God to do the things that we had not had the strength or desire to do before. We began to change our lifestyle by reading the Word of God and talking to Jesus in our new language. We needed this in order for us to be able to grow in our understanding of the Word, to have strength to overcome the devil's plans for our life, to be taught by the Spirit the wisdom of God, and to be led daily by God through the Holy Spirit. What we were experiencing was the very same experience that happened to the 120 followers who were waiting for the promise.

Jesus told the disciples in Luke 24:49, *"And behold I send the promise of my Father upon you: but tarry ye in the city of Jerusalem until ye be endued with power from on high."* Then in Acts 1:4-5, again Jesus says, *"Wait for the promise of the Father, which saith he, ye have heard of me. For John truly baptized with water, but ye shall be baptized with the Holy Ghost not many days hence."* He continues in verse 8, *"But ye shall receive power, after that the Holy Ghost is come upon you: and ye shall be witnesses unto me both in Jerusalem, and in all Judaea, and in Samaria, and unto the uttermost part of the earth."*

What is this Baptism of the Holy Spirit? It is a definite experience in which the Holy Spirit, who is already dwelling within the believer, is released to empower our life. It is administered by Jesus and is to be received by faith. It is the same transforming event that the first disciples experienced on the day of Pentecost, as described in Acts 2:1-4, *"And* when the day of Pentecost was fully come, they were all with one accord in one place. And suddenly there came a sound from heaven as of a rushing mighty wind and it filled all the house where they were sitting. And there appeared unto them cloven tongues like as of fire, and it sat upon each of them. And they were all filled with the Holy Ghost and began to speak with other tongues, as the Spirit gave them utterance." Jesus sent the Holy Spirit to us to be our guide, our helper, our comforter, and our teacher so that we could begin to manifest the Kingdom of God in our lives. The Holy Spirit indwells us and gives us the strength to be a doer of the Word of God.

There are several things you need to understand about the Baptism of the Holy Spirit.

1. <u>IT IS PROMISED TO EVERY CHRISTIAN.</u> In Acts 2:38-39, we read: *"For the promise is unto you, and to your children, and to all that are afar off, even as many as the Lord our God shall call."*

From this verse we know that the promise is the same promise that Jesus told the disciples to tarry for in Jerusalem and received on the day of Pentecost.

2. <u>IT IS A GIFT.</u> We do not have to beg for it. We cannot work for it. We cannot make ourselves good enough to receive it. It is a gift and we must receive it like we would receive any gift. We ask and receive and then take it by faith and say, "Thank You!"

3. <u>IT IS ADMINISTERED BY JESUS.</u> In Luke 3:16, we read: *"John answered, saying unto them all, I indeed baptize you*

with water; but one mightier than I cometh, the latchet of whose shoes I am not worthy to unloose; He shall baptize you with the Holy Ghost and with fire."

There is a baptism in water administered by man. There is a baptism into the Body of Christ administered by the Holy Spirit (1 Corinthians 12:13). There is also a Baptism in the Holy Spirit administered by Jesus.

In Acts 1:4, Jesus emphasized the importance of being Baptized in the Holy Spirit, and ten days later it happened on the day of Pentecost. Receiving the Holy Spirit upon conversion and being Baptized in the Holy Spirit may be two separate distinct experiences. The disciples had received the Holy Spirit on the day of Resurrection as described in John 20:22, *"And when He (Jesus) had said this, he breathed on them, and saith unto them, Receive ye the Holy Spirit."* Fifty days later they received the Baptism in the Holy Spirit. In Acts Chapter 8, the Samaritans had been baptized in water after having believed in Jesus, and yet later on they received the Baptism in the Holy Spirit when Peter and John prayed for them and laid their hands on them.

4. IT IS GOD'S WILL FOR YOU TO RECEIVE IT. In Ephesians 5:18, God commands us to be filled with the Holy Spirit. When you pray for the Baptism in the Holy Spirit you know that you are asking according to the will of God. Therefore, you can know that God will hear and answer your prayer. So ask believing that you will receive the moment you ask!

"And this is the confidence that we have in him, that, if

we ask anything according to his will, he heareth us; and if we know that he hears us, whatsoever we ask, we know that we have the petitions that we desired of him." 1 John 5:14-15.

Matthew 7:7-11, *"Ask and it shall be given you; seek, and ye shall find; knock, and it shall be opened unto you. For everyone that asketh receiveth, and he that seeketh findeth; and to him that knocketh it shall be opened. Or what man is there of you whom if his son ask bread, will he give a stone? Or if he ask a fish, will he give him a serpent? If ye then, being evil, know how to give good gifts unto your children, how much more shall your heavenly Father which is in heaven give good things to them that ask him?"*

Just receive it by faith! It is not enough to pray for the Baptism of the Holy Spirit. Some people pray for years for the Baptism and do not receive it. Why, because they do not claim it by faith. Just ask for it, receive it, and accept that you now have it because the Word of God says if you ask, you will receive. Then by faith ask God to fill your mouth with your new heavenly language. This is our language from heaven because we are now in the Kingdom of God. We have a new King in our lives, a new country, a new language, and many new things to learn about our King.

RESULTS OF THE BAPTISM OF THE HOLY SPIRIT

The Baptism of the Holy Spirit is a supernatural endowment with power from heaven that equips the Christian for effective witness and service. It is attested by speaking in a language given by the Holy Spirit, but unknown to the one speaking. It enables the Christian to build up his own spiritual life in which both the gifts and the fruits of the Holy Spirit should be manifested. In the New Testament church, this experience was considered normal for all believers. We often see the terms *"filled with the Holy Ghost"* or *"filled with the Holy Spirit."* Both carry exactly the same meaning, identifying the work of the Spirit of God.

They heard the Word and received the Baptism of the Holy Spirit.

1. <u>Received Baptism and new language.</u> On the Day of Pentecost, the disciples were in one place with one accord and began to speak with other tongues after receiving the infilling of the Holy Ghost. Acts 2:4, *"And they were all filled with the Holy Ghost, and began to speak with other tongues, as the Spirit gave them utterance."* They simply received the Holy Ghost and immediately, empowered by the Holy Spirit, began to speak in a new language.

2. <u>Laid hands on them and they received.</u> We see another example of the Samaritans hearing the Word of God, and later Peter and John being sent that they might receive the Holy Ghost. This is found in Acts 8:15, *"Who, when they were come down, prayed for them, that they might receive the Holy Ghost: For as yet he was fallen upon none of them: only they were baptized in the name of the Lord Jesus. Then laid they their hands on them and they received the Holy Ghost."* These believers simply re-

ceived by asking for the Holy Ghost and then had hands laid on them. Although it does not say that they spoke in tongues, Simon, who had been a sorcerer but was now a believer, desired to buy this gift for money that he might have this power in his life. So, he had to have seen something outwardly manifesting through these Samaritan believers.

3. <u>Laid hands on him and he received.</u> Paul also received the Holy Spirit through the laying on of hands. The account of his encounter with the Lord and then receiving can be found in Acts 9:13-19. Ananias was sent to Paul in verse 17 and laid hands on him and said, *"Receive thy sight and be filled with the Holy Ghost."* This does not mention that Paul spoke in tongues but we know from the Scripture in 1 Corinthians 14:18 Paul said, *"I thank my God, I speak with tongues more than ye all."* This is proof that Paul also spoke in tongues.

4. <u>Heard the Word and received.</u> An angel visited Cornelius in Caesarea and told him to send for a man named Peter. You can find this whole event recorded in Acts 10, thus Peter was sought out by men who took him back to Cornelius. While Peter preached to the house of Cornelius, *"The Holy Ghost fell on all them which heard the word. And they of the circumcision which believed were astonished, as many as came with Peter, because that on the Gentiles also was poured out the gift of the Holy Ghost. For they heard them speak with tongues and magnify God"* (Acts 10:44-46).

5. <u>Laid hands on them and they received.</u> Paul went to Ephesus about 20 years after Jesus' resurrection where he found disciples, which means that they were already believers. He asked them, *"Have ye received the Holy Ghost since ye believed? And they said unto him, we have not so much as heard whether there be any Holy Ghost"* (Acts 19:2) and then in verse 6, *"And when Paul had laid his hands upon them, the Holy Ghost came on them; and they spake with tongues, and prophesied."* As we can see, sometimes the gift was received by the laying on of hands, and other times, it was received by hearing the preaching of the Word. Through this gift these disciples, or believers, spoke with tongues because that is the language of the Holy Spirit. When God indwells us, He gives us a way to communicate with Him perfectly and that is our heavenly language.

6. *"So I say to you, ask, and it will be given to you; seek, and you will find; knock, and it will be opened to you. For everyone who asks receives, and he who seeks finds, and to him who knocks it will be opened. If a son asks for bread from any father among you, will he give him a stone? Or if he asks for a fish, will he give him a serpent instead of a fish? Or if he asks for an egg, will he offer him a scorpion? If you then, being evil, know how to give good gifts to your children, how much more will your heavenly Father give the Holy Spirit to those who ask Him?"* Luke 11:9-13.

WALKING IN THE SPIRIT

In order to live a constant and consistent Spirit-filled life, we must observe the following:

1. WALK BY FAITH! Do not depend on your feelings or emotions! *"We walk by faith and not by sight"* (2 Corinthians 5:7). Claim the infilling of the Holy Spirit by faith whether you feel spiritual or not. Put your faith out in front of you. Your feelings will line up with your faith.

2. CONFESS SINS INSTANTLY! Unconfessed sin in your life will grieve the Spirit; and you will lose your joy and power. Instant confession brings instant restoration.

3. ACT YOUR FAITH! Step out by faith and do the impossible. We will never know the resources of God until we attempt the impossible. Witness for Christ. Pray for the sick and expect healing. Say, "Yes" to opportunities to serve Jesus. Remember, *"Faith without works is DEAD"* (James 1:22).

4. CONFESS GOD'S WORD – NOT YOUR DOUBTS! Satan is the author of doubt and fear. Fill your heart with the Word of God. *"Resist the devil and he will flee from you"* (James 4:7). Speak what God says about your situation.

5. PRAISE GOD IN EVERYTHING THAT HAPPENS TO YOU! *"In everything give thanks"* (1 Thessalonians 5:18). Make it a habit of life to thank God in your problems as well as for your blessings. It will change your life. Know that what

you are going through on earth is preparing you for heaven. Things happen to draw us closer to God. *"Many are the afflictions of the righteous but the Lord delivereth him out of them all"* (Psalm 34:19).

6. BE AVAILABLE! The Lord will use a yielded vessel. Get involved! Become active in ministering to others. You have received the Baptism of the Holy Spirit not only to bless and enrich your own life, but also to provide a channel through which God can touch and transform the lives of others.

7. SPEND TIME ALONE WITH GOD! *"And He (Jesus) withdrew Himself into the wilderness and prayed"* (Luke 5:16).

Praying and meditating on the Word along with fasting is a powerful combination. Use it often, especially in times of crisis. This doesn't move God, but it does open you up to receive His Word and hear His voice. Remember, the Baptism of the Holy Spirit is simply moving into a deeper experience of the reality of Jesus.

PURPOSE OF TONGUES

As we look further at what the Scriptures say about speaking in an unknown tongue, we will help you see the total purpose of tongues. *"And these signs will follow those who believe: In My name they will cast out demons; they will speak with new tongues; they will take up serpents; and if they drink anything deadly, it will be no means hurt them; they will lay hands on the sick, and they will recover"* Mark 16:17-18.

1. <u>SPEAKING TO GOD.</u> We are speaking to God as 1 Corinthians 14:2 indicates, *"For he that speaketh in an unknown tongue speaketh not unto men; but unto God: for no man understandeth him; howbeit in the Spirit he speaketh mysteries."* Since we understand English, or our native language, we know that speaking to God in the Spirit is not praying quietly to him in English. *"Because the foolishness of God is wiser than men, and the weakness of God is stronger than men"* I Corinthians 1:25.

2. PRAISING AND MAGNIFYING GOD. Acts 10:46 says, *"They heard them speak with tongues and magnify God."* John 4:23-24 says, *"When the true worshippers shall worship the Father in spirit and in truth: for the Father seeketh such to worship him. God is a Spirit: and they that worship him must worship him in spirit and in truth."* We have been given this language to worship and praise God in.

3. EDIFYING YOURSELF. *"He that speaketh in an unknown tongue edifieth himself; but he that prophesieth edifieth the church"* (1 Corinthians 14: 4). This makes it clear that we are speaking directly to God as a prayer or praise and are building ourselves up or instructing ourselves. The Holy Ghost within us is teaching us, refreshing us and ministering to our needs when we pray in tongues. When we pray in tongues, our spirit is praying and we don't understand what we are saying because it is not a known language to us according to 1 Corinthians 14:14. Because it is our spirit that is praying or praising, we know we are contacting God in the Spirit. Therefore, we are speaking to God in our unknown tongue. Now in Jude 20 the

Scripture tells us that we're *"Building ourselves up on our most holy faith, praying in the Holy Ghost."* This Scripture tells us we are praying in the Holy Ghost or Holy Spirit.

4. ONE OF THE NINE GIFTS. One of the gifts of the Spirit is tongues and another is interpretation of tongues. God tells us we are to pray for the interpretation of this unknown tongue. 1 Corinthians 14:13, *"Wherefore let him that speaketh in an unknown tongue pray that he may interpret."* Also in 1 Corinthians 14:5, *"I will pray with the spirit and I will pray with the understanding,"* so that the church may receive edification when it is used as a gift in the church.

OBJECTIONS TO TONGUES

Many mainstream churches oppose the gift of tongues. Below I list some of the widespread objections that traditional churches say about speaking in tongues (these are the emboldened statements) and provide the Scripture or Scriptures that disproves the statement.

I forbid you to speak in tongues.

"Wherefore, brethren, covet to prophesy, and forbid not to speak with tongues" (1 Corinthians 14:39).

Speaking in tongues is a sign of over-emotionalism.

"And these signs shall follow them that believe; In my name shall they cast out devils; they shall speak with new tongues"

(Mark 16:17). This scripture states tongues are a sign for those that believe!

Speaking in tongues is speaking in a known, foreign language.

"For he that speaketh in an unknown tongue speaketh not unto men, but unto God: for no man understandeth him; howbeit in the spirit he speaketh mysteries" (1 Corinthians 14:2).

I'm embarrassed to speak in tongues.

"For whosoever shall be ashamed of me and of my words, of him shall the Son of man be ashamed, when he shall come in his own glory, and in his Father's, and of the holy angels" (Luke 9:26).

Tongues is of the devil.

"And they were all filled with the Holy Ghost, and began to speak with other tongues, as the Spirit gave them utterance" (Acts 2:4).

"For he that speaketh in an unknown tongue speaketh not unto men, but unto God: for no man understandeth him; howbeit in the spirit he speaketh mysteries" (1 Corinthians 14:2).

They magnify themselves, not God.

"For they heard them speak with tongues, and magnify God" (Acts 10:46).

Tongues are just for Pentecost.

This statement is not accurate. The following account happened between 12-20 years after Pentecost.

"And it came to pass, that, while Apollos was at Corinth, Paul having passed through the upper coasts came to Ephesus: and finding certain disciples, He said unto them, Have ye received the Holy Ghost since ye believed? And they said unto him, We have not so much as heard whether there be any Holy Ghost. And he said unto them, Unto what then were ye baptized? And they said, Unto John's baptism. Then said Paul, John verily baptized with the baptism of repentance, saying unto the people, that they should believe on him which should come after him, that is, on Christ Jesus. When they heard this, they were baptized in the name of the Lord Jesus. And when Paul had laid his hands upon them, the Holy Ghost came on them; and they spake with tongues, and prophesied" (Acts 19:1-6).

Tongues ceased with the Apostles.

"Charity never faileth: but whether there be prophecies, they shall fail; whether there be tongues, they shall cease; whether there be knowledge, it shall vanish away. For we know in part, and we prophesy in part. But when that which is perfect is come, then that which is in part shall be done away. When I was a child, I spake as a child, I understood as a child, I thought as a child: but when I became a man, I put away childish things. For now we see through a glass, darkly; but then face to face: now I know in part; but then shall I know even as also I am known" (1 Corinthians 13:8-12). Some teach that the perfect we are face to face with is the Bible. But, has knowledge vanished away or stopped? No, it hasn't. Knowledge continues to increase; therefore, that which is perfect is when we are face to face with Jesus. Then we won't need prophecy or tongues and interpretations.

Speaking in tongues doesn't do any good.

"For he that speaketh in an unknown tongue speaketh not unto men, but unto God: for no man understandeth him; howbeit in the spirit he speaketh mysteries. But he that prophesieth speaketh unto men to edification, and exhortation, and comfort. He that speaketh in an unknown tongue edifieth himself; but he that prophesieth edifieth the church" (1 Corinthians 14:2-4). The word "edify" means to build one up. So speaking in tongues builds us up in the "most holy faith" Jude 20.

"I would that ye all spake with tongues but rather that ye prophesied: for greater is he that prophesieth than he that speaketh with tongues, except he interpret, that the church may receive edifying. Now, brethren, if I come unto you speaking with tongues, what shall I profit you, except I shall speak to you either by revelation, or by knowledge, or by prophesying, or by doctrine? And even things without life giving sound, whether pipe or harp, except they give a distinction in the sounds, how shall it be known what is piped or harped? For if the trumpet give an uncertain sound, who shall prepare himself to the battle? So likewise ye, except ye utter by the tongue words easy to be understood, how shall it be known what is spoken? for ye shall speak into the air. There are, it may be, so many kinds of voices in the world, and none of them is without signification. Therefore if I know not the meaning of the voice, I shall be unto him that speaketh a barbarian, and he that speaketh shall be a barbarian unto me. Even so ye, forasmuch as ye are zealous of spiritual gifts, seek that ye may excel to the edifying of the church.

Wherefore let him that speaketh in an unknown tongue pray that he may interpret. For if I pray in an unknown tongue, my spirit prayeth, but my understanding is unfruitful. What is it then? I will pray with the spirit, and I will pray with the understanding also: I will sing with the spirit, and I will sing with the understanding also. Else when thou shalt bless with the spirit, how shall he that occupieth the room of the unlearned say Amen at thy giving of thanks, seeing he understandeth not what thou sayest? For thou verily givest thanks well, but the other is not edified. I thank my God, I speak with tongues more than ye all: Yet in the church I had rather speak five words with my understanding, that by my voice I might teach others also, than ten thousand words in an unknown tongue. Brethren, be not children in understanding: howbeit in malice be ye children, but in understanding be men. In the law it is written, With men of other tongues and other lips will I speak unto this people; and yet for all that will they not hear me, saith the Lord. Wherefore tongues are for a sign, not to them that believe, but to them that believe not: but prophesying serveth not for them that believe not, but for them which believe" (1 Corinthians 14:5-22).

"But ye, beloved, building up yourselves on your most holy faith, praying in the Holy Ghost" (Jude 1:20).

I would be kicked out of my church if I did.

"For they loved the praise of men more than the praise of God" (John 12:43). Many churches are led of men and not of the Spirit of God. To them many of the things of God are foolishness. We are not to please men but Him that called us!

A missionary in Africa heard people cursing God in tongues.

"Wherefore I give you to understand, that no man speaking by the Spirit of God calleth Jesus accursed: and that no man can say that Jesus is the Lord, but by the Holy Ghost" (1 Corinthians 12:3).

Tongues were given to just the Apostles.

"And there was a certain disciple at Damascus, named Ananias; and to him said the Lord in a vision, Ananias. And he said, Behold, I am here, Lord. And the Lord said unto him, Arise, and go into the street which is called Straight, and enquire in the house of Judas for one called Saul, of Tarsus: for, behold, he prayeth, And hath seen in a vision a man named Ananias coming in, and putting his hand on him, that he might receive his sight. Then Ananias answered, Lord, I have heard by many of this man, how much evil he hath done to thy saints at Jerusalem: And here he hath authority from the chief priests to bind all that call on thy name. But the Lord said unto him, Go thy way: for he is a chosen vessel unto me, to bear my name before the Gentiles, and kings, and the children of Israel: For I will shew him how great things he must suffer for my name's sake. And Ananias went his way, and entered into the house; and putting his hands on him said, Brother Saul, the Lord, even Jesus, that appeared unto thee in the way as thou camest, hath sent me, that thou mightest receive thy sight, and be filled with the Holy Ghost" (Acts 9:10-17).

I got it all in one experience.

"Then Philip went down to the city of Samaria, and preached

Christ unto them. And the people with one accord gave heed unto those things which Philip spake, hearing and seeing the miracles which he did. For unclean spirits, crying with loud voice, came out of many that were possessed with them: and many taken with palsies, and that were lame, were healed. And there was great joy in that city. But there was a certain man, called Simon, which beforetime in the same city used sorcery, and bewitched the people of Samaria, giving out that himself was some great one: To whom they all gave heed, from the least to the greatest, saying, This man is the great power of God. And to him they had regard, because that of long time he had bewitched them with sorceries. But when they believed Philip preaching the things concerning the kingdom of God, and the name of Jesus Christ, they were baptized, both men and women. Then Simon himself believed also: and when he was baptized, he continued with Philip, and wondered, beholding the miracles and signs which were done. Now when the apostles which were at Jerusalem heard that Samaria had received the word of God, they sent unto them Peter and John: Who, when they were come down, prayed for them, that they might receive the Holy Ghost: (For as yet he was fallen upon none of them: only they were baptized in the name of the Lord Jesus). Then laid they their hands on them, and they received the Holy Ghost" (Acts 8:5-17).

"And it came to pass, that, while Apollos was at Corinth, Paul having passed through the upper coasts came to Ephesus: and finding certain disciples, He said unto them, Have ye received the Holy Ghost since ye believed? And they said unto him, We have not so much as heard whether there be any Holy Ghost.

And he said unto them, Unto what then were ye baptized? And they said, Unto John's baptism. Then said Paul, John verily baptized with the baptism of repentance, saying unto the people, that they should believe on him which should come after him, that is, on Christ Jesus. When they heard this, they were baptized in the name of the Lord Jesus. And when Paul had laid his hands upon them, the Holy Ghost came on them; and they spake with tongues, and prophesied" (Acts 19:1-6). In verse two Paul made an unusual statement, *"Have ye received the Holy Ghost SINCE YE BELIEVED."* This shows that the experience of the Baptism of the Holy Spirit can be a separate experience after you believe.

Tongues is not a part of the church service.

"I would that ye all spake with tongues but rather that ye prophesied: for greater is he that prophesieth than he that speaketh with tongues, except he interpret, that the church may receive edifying" (1 Corinthians 14:5). Tongues, when interpreted, is equal in the service to prophecy, and is part of the service.

Paul said he'd rather speak five words in English than 10,000 words in tongues in the church. *"I thank my God, I speak with tongues more than ye all"* (1 Corinthians 14:18).

I can pray in the Spirit without praying in tongues.

"For if I pray in an unknown tongue, my spirit prayeth, but my understanding is unfruitful" (1 Corinthians 14:14). Paul is saying that when we pray in the Spirit we are praying in tongues. There is no other area of scripture that states another way to pray in the Spirit.

Not everyone can speak in tongues.

"I would that ye all spake with tongues but rather that ye prophesied: for greater is he that prophesieth than he that speaketh with tongues, except he interpret, that the church may receive edifying" (1 Corinthians 14:5).

"And these signs shall follow them that believe; In my name shall they cast out devils; they shall speak with new tongues" (Mark 16:17).

"Then Peter said unto them, Repent, and be baptized every one of you in the name of Jesus Christ for the remission of sins, and ye shall receive the gift of the Holy Ghost. For the promise is unto you, and to your children, and to all that are afar off, even as many as the LORD our God shall call" (Acts 2:38-39).

If it's of God, you don't need to teach and instruct people about it.

"This only would I learn of you, Received ye the Spirit by the works of the law, or by the hearing of faith?" (Galatians 3:2).

'So then faith cometh by hearing, and hearing by the word of God" (Romans 10:17).

I saw people who were in the flesh.

"And it shall come to pass in the last days, saith God, I will pour out of my Spirit upon all flesh: and your sons and your daughters shall prophesy, and your young men shall see visions, and your old men shall dream dreams" (Acts 2:17). Some state it is just emotionalism—this is true. We are emotional beings and when the reality of the greatness and

goodness of God enters our life, we get emotional. Yes, our flesh gets excited about God. The outward manifestation can come in many ways: tears of joy, laughter, shouting, and dancing about. How it will be manifested is totally dependent upon the individual.

What good is speaking in tongues?

I have provided six reasons below to illustrate just how beneficial tongues are to the believer's walk with God.

1. Praise and Magnify God

   "To him give all the prophets witness, that through his name whosoever believeth in him shall receive remission of sins. While Peter yet spake these words, the Holy Ghost fell on all them which heard the word. And they of the circumcision which believed were astonished, as many as came with Peter, because that on the Gentiles also was poured out the gift of the Holy Ghost. For they heard them speak with tongues and magnify God" (Acts 10:43-46).

   "For he that speaketh in an unknown tongue speaketh not unto men, but unto God: for no man understandeth him; howbeit in the spirit he speaketh mysteries" (1 Corinthians 14:2). No wonder man in the natural does not understand, because we are speaking directly to God and not man.

2. Pray perfectly

   "Likewise the Spirit also helpeth our infirmities: for we

know not what we should pray for as we ought: but the Spirit itself maketh intercession for us with groanings which cannot be uttered. And he that searcheth the hearts knoweth what is the mind of the Spirit, because he maketh intercession for the saints according to the will of God" (Romans 8:26-27). The Spirit of God knows God's plan for our lives and speaks the will of God into existence in the language of God. This is just like in Genesis 1 where God spoke creation into existence, *"God said."* This same Spirit of confession is working through us when we allow Him to speak His will through us in the language of heaven.

3. Intercede for others

   See Romans 8:26-27 above

4. Rest and refreshing

   "For with stammering lips and another tongue will he speak to this people. To whom he said, This is the rest wherewith ye may cause the weary to rest; and this is the refreshing: yet they would not hear" (Isaiah 28:11-12). God speaks His will through us when we allow the Holy Spirit of God to speak through us. This builds up our faith and speaks forth the will of God for our lives. Meanwhile, praying this way allows us to enter into His rest knowing He has everything under control.

5. Allows your spirit to pray

   "For if I pray in an unknown tongue, my spirit pray-

eth, but my understanding is unfruitful. What is it then? I will pray with the spirit, and I will pray with the understanding also: I will sing with the spirit, and I will sing with the understanding also" (I Corinthians 14:14-15).

6. Edifies one's self

"He that speaketh in an unknown tongue edifieth himself; but he that prophesieth edifieth the church" (I Corinthians 14:4). The word edify means to build up. When we pray in tongues we are "building up ourselves in our most holy faith."

PRAYER TO RECEIVE THE BAPTISM OF THE HOLY SPIRIT

Here is a prayer that you can pray to receive the Baptism of the Holy Spirit.

Dear God, Thank you for sending your son Jesus to the earth to die for my sins. I have accepted Jesus as my Lord and Saviour. I now ask for the Baptism of the Holy Spirit. I receive the Baptism by faith right now. Lord, I also ask that you would now fill my mouth with my new language and allow it to come forth out of my spirit right now. Thank you, and I ask all of this in the Name of Jesus. Amen.

Now, as an expression of your faith that God has heard and answered your prayer, just begin to praise Him, but do not speak in your own language. Many times, I tell people to take a deep breath and breathe in the Holy Spirit and when they breathe out, just let the Holy Spirit do the talking. This language bypasses your mind. You cannot think of the words, you just have to open your mouth and by faith the words come out. But, you have to OPEN YOUR MOUTH and TALK, but not in English or your native tongue. I have led many people in receiving the Baptism and many won't open their mouths to say anything. They think God will force their mouths open and put words in their mouths, but God won't force it on you. You have to desire it and by faith receive, and open your mouth to allow his new language to come forth. Here are four facts showing the importance of this language from God.

1. You are offering perfect praise to God in the Spirit.

2. You will be cooperating with God in a spiritual miracle.

3. It will give you a hotline to heaven.

4. It will edify you and build you up.

The Baptism in the Holy Spirit will bring many changes into your life, including the following:

1. Jesus Christ will become more real and personal to you than ever before.

2. As you read the Bible, God will speak to you more clearly. You will find its truths more meaningful. You will have a greater desire to read it.

3. You will feel love for others flowing through your life such as you have never experienced.

4. You will begin to experience miracles day by day as you maintain a Spirit-filled life.

5. You will have a desire to begin ministering to others.

6. It will be easier for you to share Christ with those who do not know Him. You will have a new power and desire in witnessing for Him.

7. As you open up your life fully to the ministry of the Holy Spirit, you will be used in spiritual gifts such as: Healing, Miracles, Prophecy, Tongues, Interpretations of Tongues, Words of Knowledge, Words of Wisdom, etc. (For more on spiritual gifts, see 1 Corinthians, Chapter 12 and 14; and also Romans 12).

Now that you have received the Baptism of the Holy Spirit by faith, it is important to walk in the Spirit moment by moment. Ephesians 5:18 says, *"Be filled with the Spirit."* In the original Greek it says, *"keep being filled"* or "be constantly filled with the Holy Spirit." This simply means that we are not to rely upon a one-time experience, but daily we are to experience fresh fillings and the anointing of the Spirit.

NINE GIFTS OF THE SPIRIT

Paul tells us that God would not have us ignorant concerning Spiritual gifts in 1 Corinthians 12:1. He wants us to know and understand the workings of the gifts that we have received. There are nine gifts of the spirit given to profit us. 1 Corinthians 12:8-11, *"For to one is given by the Spirit the word of wisdom; to another the word of knowledge by the same Spirit; To another faith by the same Spirit; to another the gifts of healing by the same Spirit; to another the working of miracles; to another prophecy; to another discerning of spirits; to another divers kinds of tongues; to another the interpretation of tongues: But all these worketh that one and the selfsame Spirit dividing to every man severally as he will."* The Holy Spirit gives the necessary gift or gifts to the believer in his point of need. These gifts are a result of receiving the Baptism of the Holy Spirit. God's plan is that we operate in these gifts to improve our lives; to give us wisdom and knowledge, to help us step out in faith, to receive healing, to perform miracles, to prophecy, to have discernment of the spiritual world, and to have the benefit of tongues and interpretation.

In 1 Corinthians 14:1, Paul tells us to follow after charity or love and desire spiritual gifts, but mostly desire that you may prophesy as this edifies the body of Christ. 1 Corinthians 13:1-2, *"Though I speak with the tongues of men and of angels, and have not charity, I am become as sounding brass, or a tinkling cymbal. And though I have the gift of prophecy, and understand all mysteries, and all knowledge; and though I have all faith, so that I could remove mountains, and have not charity, I am nothing."*

FRUIT OF THE SPIRIT

The fruit of the Spirit is listed in Galatians 5:22, *"But the fruit of the Spirit is love, joy, peace, longsuffering, gentleness, goodness, faith, meekness, temperance: against such there is no law."* God desires that we crucify the fleshly affections and lusts and begin to allow the Spirit to manifest these fruits in our lives as we walk and live in the Spirit.

PROPHECY, DREAMS, AND VISIONS

There are three supernatural occurrences that will result from the outpouring of the Holy Spirit at the end of this age found in Acts 2:17, *"And it shall come to pass in the last days, saith God, "I will pour out of my Spirit upon all flesh; and your sons and your daughters shall prophesy,* (using one's voice to speak the things of God) *and your young men shall see visions, and your old men shall dream dreams."* This was prophesied by Joel and began when Jesus sent the Holy Spirit back upon those waiting in the upper room. Joel 2:28, *"And it shall come to pass afterward that I will pour out My Spirit on all flesh; Your sons and your daughters shall prophesy, Your old men shall dream dreams, Your young men shall see visions."*

THE LANGUAGE OF THE KINGDOM OF GOD

Not only does the Baptism of the Holy Spirit loose God's great power to His citizens in the Kingdom of God, it gives us a new language—the language of heaven, a prayer language, a Spirit language by which we can communicate directly and perfectly to God our Father. As citizens in the Kingdom of

God, we should not be surprised that our citizenship would include receiving a new language—tongues are the language of the Kingdom of God. And God richly blesses us with the ability to speak His language when we humble ourselves before Him and speak out in faith. Once you have the gift of tongues, you will be a stronger, more effective citizen in the Kingdom of God.

CHAPTER 4

WALKING IN THE KINGDOM OF GOD

Much of what we have learned here on earth about life is the instruction we received early on from our parents. For example, many of us grew up with parents who were disciplinarians that would direct our actions by discipline to meet their approval. They would say, "Here's what you do—you don't cross the street here, you don't do this, or you don't do that." And there were natural consequences for not obeying or meeting their expectations. They instructed us and directed us to grow up, go through school, sports, military, or whatever, to become acclimated to a point where we could start living our own lives; and we were to become productive members of society no longer being dependent upon them. It is only when we are left to ourselves without direction and support or real responsibility that we end up in trouble, thus the admonition that we are to assemble ourselves together as the church. Likewise, when we become born again and receive the Baptism of the Holy Spirit, the Spirit of God starts to live in our hearts and the Holy Spirit begins to instruct and direct us.

So we begin this journey of "How do we live success-fully in the Kingdom of God?" Now that we are citizens of the Kingdom of God, now that we have the power of the Baptism of the Holy Spirit and the language of heaven, we have our passport to the Kingdom of God, right? Not so fast. We haven't arrived quite yet. I want to share with you what the Bible teaches us about walking in the Kingdom of God, and it is in stark contrast to the many churches that have established doctrines that say, "If you do this, and you do that, you are going to be okay." I remember the first church we attended after receiving Jesus and the Baptism. We received an attendance card that also listed 10 or more things that we would not or should not do anymore to become members. We were so excited about pleasing God that we maxed out the card in the first week since we were able to say, "We don't drink, we don't smoke, we don't go to movies, we don't swear, we don't dance, we don't play board games, we don't play cards, we don't have records that are worldly," etc. Then, all of a sudden, our Christianity was based on the fact that our membership card was filled out—all 10 of those things were done. I do believe that this could represent the fruit of a separated life and should be a moral compass, but this doesn't represent what God is asking of the church. What's left? Do we spend the rest of our Christian lives going around, saying, "Wow, I have arrived," and judging everybody else for how they're dressed or what they are doing or not doing? Amen or oh me? Is this pretty close? It really is in denominational churches. I was confirmed at the age of 13 and thought I was going to heaven. I don't think so! There is more to it than we, as individuals, have been taught. I know there is a vital link to heavenly God through Jesus Christ, that He wants to use our life for His purpose on this earth—not us use Him for our purpose. Acts 4:12, *"Neither is there salvation in any other: for there is none other name under heaven given among men, whereby we must be saved."*

The bottom line about walking in the Kingdom of God is not arriving at a destination or having your membership card maxed out. It is living out a real relationship with almighty God and letting Him live His life through us. How do we do that? There are several key processes and transitions that must take place in order for us to obediently walk in the Kingdom of God.

RENEWING OUR MIND

One of the first transitions that must occur is the renewing of our minds. We begin our walk with God and that walk is the casting off of who we are—our will, our way, our desires—and saying, "God, I don't care about what I want, I am going to follow you." Then we begin this process of growing spiritually. We begin to talk to God, read His Word, learn all about who Jesus is and what He did for us. The Bible tells us to renew our minds in Romans 12:2, *"And be not conformed to this world: but be ye transformed by the renewing of your mind, that ye may prove what is that good and acceptable, and perfect, will of God."* I read the Bible through, cover to cover, in a 3-month period after I was born again and baptized in the Holy Spirit. Why? Because I wanted to know the truth, and

I was consumed with understanding spiritual things. I started to renew my mind by mediating on God's Word. Ephesians 4:23 says, *"And be renewed in the spirit of your mind"* along with Colossians 3:10 telling us to, *"Put on the new man."* Both of these Scriptures are followed by other commands of what we are to put off or to die to, such as lying, stealing, corrupt communication, anger, wrath, and any evil work. The Word then lists what we are to put on or how we are to change by renewing our minds. Learning how to love, to forgive, be kind, be patient, and to have peace are a few. As I studied, I found out that God asks us to do the impossible through the improbable powered by the invisible. That really bothered me because I knew that there was nothing in my background that would allow me to do any of those things. In addition, God is inaudible most of the time when you really need to hear from him because He wants us to live by faith. His Word says, *"He has given us all things that pertain unto life and godliness, through the knowledge of him."* The Word of God reveals God's knowledge and wisdom, *"That hath called us to glory and virtue"* (2 Peter 1:3).

MEDITATING THE WORD

How do we begin this process of renewing our minds and living by faith and not by sight or what we see, hear and feel? We begin by meditating the Word as Joshua 1:8 says, *"This book of the law shall not depart out of thy mouth; but thou shalt meditate therein day and night that thou mayest observe to do according to all that is written therein: for then thou shalt make thy way prosperous, and then thou shalt have good success."* Meditating the word is as simple as thinking about certain Scriptures and mulling them over and over in your mind. That is how we will have good success. Some people think that to meditate we have to sit on the floor, get in a yoga position and then think real hard about a particular Scripture. Meditating is as simple as thinking on whatever thoughts cross your brain during a normal day. If you can then begin to worry about one of these thoughts, you have begun to meditate on whatever those worrisome thoughts are. So we need to focus on Scriptures and think upon them during the day. The Word of God has to be our main focus, knowing what the Word says and learning all of His ways. Who creates the prosperity? We do—through the knowledge of the Word, Joshua 1:8, *'then thou shall make thy way prosperous.'* As we profit in the things of God, we are convinced in the ways of God, and our life starts to become successful. I identify this as doing God's will. Why? The reason is now we have the faith to wait on God in every situation. Our impatience will give us a lot of reasons to bail out on Him, but we must stand our ground convinced of a miraculous God.

When I was first saved in 1973, I would go to Oral Roberts University to visit, and what I got out of that was "Expect a Miracle." Everybody who knows me knows that every time I go to the mailbox, I am expecting a miracle. Why? Because I believe that God, on a daily basis, works miraculously in our lives. He's there and if we don't see those little miracles, we won't see the greatness of God. Yet, He doesn't do those kinds of miracles all of the time. He does things that are so small that you have to look for them to see them. For me, this can also be by bringing people into our lives, a phone call from someone, or meeting someone during your day that may have a Word from God for you.

If you know God's Word, you are not fearful or ashamed. You are bold and you are strong, and when everything starts going sideways and upside down according to natural thinking you think, 'this has got to be God because if everything was going perfect, my faith would not have the opportunity to be exercised. Faith is the rock-solid and eternal conviction that the unseen is real. That means that God's promises are real to me. He said that, *"Wherever I put my foot he would give me that land;"* that *"No weapon formed against me would prosper;"* that *"I am more than a conqueror"* in the things I go through; he would always *"Give me a way of escape"* (1 Corinthians 10:13) and that *"I could do all things through him because he will strengthen me"* (Philippians 4:13).

In the book of Jude, he told people to press in and return to the original faith that was once given to them, and that was a mere 40 years after Christ had died for them. There is a process of deception that is coming into the church, into the world, from even the very beginning of time, of Satan's ability to separate mankind from a vital, living relationship with God. Satan has tried to destroy the integrity of God's Word for the purpose of destroying God's people and sending all earthly beings to hell without a revelation of God, without being truly born again. So we must *"know the truth and the truth will set us free"* (John 8:32). As you find truth, you begin to know that the God you serve is the greatest God and the only God, and that *"He has come to give us life and more abundant life"* (John 10:10). That is the nature of God. Jesus himself died for us so that we can have the very nature and essence of God within us. So when we pray and ask God that His Kingdom would come on earth as it is in heaven, we are asking Him to come into our lives and that the Kingdom of God would become resident within us. *"I am crucified with Christ: nevertheless I live; yet not I, but Christ liveth in me: and the life which I now live in the flesh I live by the faith of the Son of God, who loved me, and gave himself for me"* (Galatians 2:20).

DIVISION OF SOUL AND SPIRIT

In Hebrews 4:12, we begin looking at the process of the division of soul and spirit. This verse talks about the Bible, the Word of God, saying, *"For the word of God is quick, powerful, and sharper than any two edged sword."* So the Word is quick, powerful, and sharper than any two-edged sword. What's the purpose? To pierce even to the dividing asunder (the Greek word is merismos) of the soul and spirit. We get our word "metamorphosis" from this Greek word. For example, we know that butterflies and tadpoles undergo a metamorphosis, or new beginning. The verse continues, *"Dividing asunder of soul and spirit, and of the joints and marrow, and is a discerner of the thoughts and intents of our heart."* So the Word of God comes into us and begins a process of dividing (merismos) our soul and spirit. Now why does it separate us? Well, it gives us revelation knowledge about who God is. Remember when you were born again? About two or three months later you are still trying to figure out this new spiritual world you are in. Why is that? Because a revelation of God is coming into your life for the purpose of illuminating, to turn on the lights in your life, about the things of God. Prior to that you knew about God, but you didn't know God. So the Word of God begins to work within us, causing a revelation for the purpose of illuminating in us the wisdom of God and the very being of God. What else does it do? It starts a separation process. What's the separation? The separation process is separating the soul (the part that knows us) from the spirit (the part that knows God) for the purpose of clarifying within us what's happening. When we're born again, our spirit is born again and put into contact with the revelation of God. You are spiritually alive, you're illuminated, and all the lights go on. Yes! God is real, and you go around telling all your friends the first year or two and everybody gets saved, right? Why? Because you are illuminated and there is clarity within your life. You know that God is living within you. And, so you begin this process of understanding what God is doing within you.

Man is spirit, soul, and body. In the soul realm is our mind, our will, and our emotions. Our soul is that part which knows us, that's the part we must die to daily. Our soul is our human wisdom, which we were taught in school and by our parents all of our life. For clarification, we now have the spirit, which is the spirit of God, which has the mind of Christ, and the direction for our life. So our role in life is to begin to meditate upon the things of God (His Word), so that we can bring clarity to our lives about what God's will is and what His will is for us. When the Word comes alive, all of a sudden, we realize that we have to die to our purposes, take up our cross, live a resurrected life, and then begin our walk, hearing what the Spirit is saying to us. How do you do that? You walk with the revelation that you have been crucified with Christ and your life is no longer your own; it belongs to God for His purpose on this earth. He says, " I will reward you in this life and the life to come." All you have to do is trust Him and believe in Him. That's when we move into a miraculous realm with God where we have no fears anymore, and we start believing that whatever God says is true. When He says, *"go to the ends of the earth,"* the next thing you know you are headed out the door on a new journey. You're no longer afraid of losing what the world says is important because you are embracing that which is truly important; and you are so convinced that all hell cannot keep you from the blessing that God has for you, and you become truly determined in your heart. Now begins this merismos in your life, this separation. The Bible says the Spirit within us *"is a discerner of the thoughts and intents of your heart."* We have our own thoughts and intents of our heart and we have the thoughts and purposes of God within us in the Spirit. As a Christian, every thought you have is not your own because Satan and our flesh can produce wrong thoughts and emotions, and then begins the battle in our mind.

In Watchman Nee's book "The Release of the Spirit," published in China in 1955, He wrote that the path to Spiritual fruitfulness and intimate knowledge of the Lord is through the brokenness of the outer man. He wrote, "No life manifests more beauty than the one who is broken. Stubbornness and self love have given way to beauty in the one who is broken by God." In order for the Spirit to be victorious in the battle of the mind, there are several things that you need to begin to do:

1. Shut down the voices that are in there that want to cause you failure and destruction.

2. Open up your heart to hear the voice of God.

3. Harden your heart to the devil, no longer allowing the negative thoughts and purposes of Satan to guide your life.

4. Harden your heart to the flesh and no longer allow the negative thoughts and emotions (natural desires and lusts) of the flesh to guide your life.

5. Identify the source of your thoughts. Asking ourselves questions concerning the thoughts to determine whether or not they are from the Lord or the flesh, according to the Word of God.

Hardening your heart to those wrong thoughts and emotions is called spiritual warfare; this will allow the Word of God to flow through you. You will become more than conquerors in all types of situations because you know what you believe! You're going to stand and you're going to be bold and strong—you're not going to let defeat and failure become a part of your life in any area because of Jesus living within you. He is greater than any problem you'll ever face, He is greater than any need you'll ever have, He is greater than any financial problem you'll ever have. We've got to elevate our thinking because the Word says our God will always supply all of our needs in Christ Jesus. I remember when gas was 19 cents a gallon in 1963, and God still is supplying people's needs, no matter what the price! What we know is that God provides in every situation. I know many people that have gone through tremendous trials in the flesh, but they overcame and came out the other side, giving them conviction about what God was going to do through their life. Ephesians 6:11-16 is a good example of what we are to do, *"Put on the whole armor of God, that ye may be able to stand against the wiles of the devil. For we wrestle not against flesh and blood, but against principalities, against powers, against the rulers of the darkness of this world, against spiritual wickedness in high places. Wherefore take unto you the whole armor of God that you may be able to withstand in the evil day, and having done all, to stand. Stand therefore, having your loins (hips) girt about with truth, having put on the breastplate of righteousness, and having shod your feet with the preparation of the gospel of peace; above all taking the shield of faith with which you will be able to quench all the fiery darts of the wicked one."*

The Devil will do everything in his power to cause you to believe a lie. He doesn't want you to believe that God is going to take care of every need that you have. So he will come to you with doubts and reasonings of why God is not going to help you or take care of you. We are going to have to go to battle to receive what we know to be truth, what we know that God has promised us, and we do that by standing and standing and standing on what the Word of God says. Every time God tells me to do a greater thing, I have to go through a time of spiritual warfare in my own thought processes to get the victory; and the enemy will come and tell you how lousy you are, how it won't work, how God doesn't do that anymore, all to convince you not to press in. But, when I have pressed into God, I have seen the miracles and provisions and I have seen God do awesome things. If I backed up, I have backed up into my own ability and we all know how scary that can be. You can't back up in God. You get so far out there that the only way you can exist is God. If there were no God, I would have known that a long time ago because I have given Him every opportunity to prove Himself a failure and He never has. It is unbelievable what God does, but we have to learn there is a separation in the voices that we hear in our minds. There is one voice that is all fleshly, worldly (filled with natural wisdom) and then there is another that is all heavenly (spiritual truths), and that's the Word of God. The more you know about the Word of God, the more convinced you become of the Word of God; and the more convinced you become about the Word of God, the more you're convinced about how God operates and does miracles through His Word. That's why Paul said in Romans 8:6, *"to be carnally minded is death,"* because you're born again but trying to live your life in the flesh, and it doesn't work.

In the book of James we find an interesting Scripture in chapter 1 verse 21: *"Wherefore lay apart all filthiness and superfluity of naughtiness and receive with meekness the engrafted word, which is able to save your souls."* Verse 22 says,

"But be ye doers of the word, and not hearers only, deceiving yourself." As we meditate the Word of God it brings illumination to our minds by turning on the spiritual light that allows us to see God for who He is. This illumination produces clarity in our mind, and revelation of God's Word begins to bring separation in our lives. This can be identified as being the soul of man discovering the reality found in the Spirit of God and by our wills submitting ourselves to Him. We begin to become doers of the Word by walking away from our old lives and beginning to live in our new life by co-operating with the Spirit of God. Our lives then are transformed, and Jesus truly becomes the Lord of our lives. 2 Corinthians 4:11 says, *"For we which live are always delivered unto death for Jesus' sake, that the life also of Jesus might be made manifest in our mortal flesh."* When we live in the Spirit of God, the power of God begins to manifest Himself through our lives, as our mortal bodies become the residence of God's Spirit. It is then that we begin to cooperate with the Spirit of God in our lives, and our soul humbles itself to the leadership of the Holy Spirit. We are displaying outwardly our inner transformation, our redeemed nature. Galatians 2:20 becomes an actuality, *"For I am crucified with Christ; nevertheless I live; yet not I, but Christ liveth in me: and the life which I now live in the flesh I live by the faith of the Son of God, who loved me, and gave Himself for me."* Our ultimate goal is to be like Jesus!

The spirit and soul are separated, but when they are unified you will be able to do the will of God and not your own thing. My soul man has to yield itself to the Spirit of God; otherwise, there is a battle between my will and the will of

God. If the Spirit of God says $2 + 3 = 27$, I don't care what I think in the natural—it doesn't mean a thing. I believe God. We may not understand all the Bible, but I choose to believe it all and become a doer of what it says. If you look at how God operates through the Old Testament, you'll see that He has people doing all sorts of things that don't make sense. He had Joshua and the people walking around Jericho quietly seven times, and the seventh time they yelled at the walls so that they fell down, bringing victory to God's people. That doesn't make sense, but it's God. I have found that 9 out of 10 times when something doesn't make sense, it's God. He tells you to do the impossible and you just do it. There is no ability that you have within yourself to do anything because you are standing in faith, convinced of His goodness and His grace and His power and His ability to operate through you. And He does it all of a sudden—the Bible says, "And suddenly." You know, I live for those "And suddenly's" when I see God act because you sure go through a lot of questionable stuff along the way, and you will have every opportunity to doubt. But, the longer you stand, the more you know, the more you turn your back on the world and all the circumstances you are facing, and you realize all you need to be facing is God. When you're facing Him, everything is going to be all right, I don't care what happens. This world is not about accumulation and it's not about security, it's about heaven, a place where we are going. This time on earth is the only time we'll ever have to lay up treasure in heaven. We need to be more convinced of heaven than our worst enemies, the Muslims. We are so convinced of the world, we're like, "Whoa, I don't know if I want to trust God that much, He wants me to give my money!"

You just need to give God your life, period. It's so good then, instead of wrestling with what God wants you to do with your money you simply say, "God, thy will be done." We just have to give up our control over our provision, there is no stocking up or storing up, it's always faith in God's provision. He says, *"take no thought of tomorrow, tomorrow will take care of itself,"* so we are commanded to not worry about it. His provision is more than enough, and He provides it on a daily basis. Even when the nation of Israel was walking through the wilderness, God didn't provide a big warehouse of food so that the people could go to the grocery store and get food for a few months so that they didn't have to trust God. No, their provision was day by day. There is nothing wrong with groceries; I am just saying God wants you to look to Him for your provision on a daily basis, and see His hand of provision.

So we see that separating the old man, the soul and all your learned, natural responses, from the new man, the Spirit and God's responses, is a process. It takes renewing your mind, meditating the Word, and trusting God—not yourself—to deliver. But, how do we know when God is directing us, and we are not just acting on our own? Good question, and that is why we need to press in to know God so we know His voice and His ways. Let's continue.

PRESSING IN TO KNOW GOD

When I was a young Christian, a man told me, "Stay green and just keep growing." Being green means you're young; you don't know everything, you're teachable. That is the purpose of serving God, we all have to stay green and keep growing because we will never arrive. None of us will ever arrive. We are always on our way, and we need to press in to know the Lord. Now Paul didn't say, "It's really easy, you go to church every Sunday, you skip a few meetings, and its fine." No, he says, *"I want to press in to know the Lord."* I know with my marital relationship, I needed to press in to know my wife and she had to press in to know me. As we've done it, we've been able to come together in a relationship where we know each other. Then if someone says something about Penny or something about Dan, we can respond immediately with "no, Dan wouldn't do that" or "yes, Penny would think to do that." That's the same way you become with God. You become so convinced of who He is that you are humbled by Him. As we press in to know the Lord, we then can be led of the Lord and become doers of the Word.

Salvation is instant but conquest of the mind is progressive. The key to receiving revelations (the transfer of knowledge from the Spirit to the mind) from the Holy Spirit to be translated into action to glorify God is: to conquer the mind and bring it under the control of the Word of God. If our minds are continually controlled by Satan through fear, frustration, worry, confusion, disappointment, resentment, bitterness etc., the Holy Spirit is unable to transfer the knowledge of God to your mind.

In the New Testament, God tells us time and time again how we can discover the Spirit-filled life, how we can be led of the Lord. Romans 12:1 says, *"I beseech you therefore, brethren, by the mercies of God, that ye present your body a living sacrifice,"* (this is my body, I present it to God as a living sacrifice) *"holy, acceptable unto God, which is your reasonable service."* Well, what does that mean? It means my body becomes the vehicle for God's purposes on this earth. 1 Corinthians 6:20 says, *"My body has been bought with a price,"* it's no longer mine to do with it what I want. It is for His purpose, and this is the vehicle that God wants to use. Then he says, *"And be not conformed to this world, be transformed."* There is that word "metamorphous" again, be transformed. How can I be transformed? Read your Bible, it's only through the Word of God that we are transformed. The Bible is the biggest selling book in the world, yet it is the least read. If the spirit of slumber comes upon you and keeps you from the Word of God, you will never know the ways of God. If you don't know the Word, and don't give yourself wholly to walking it out and doing it, you will end up giving up your eternal rewards because you won't understand that God's purpose in this life is to prepare you for heaven.

And whatever happens, *"In everything give thanks for this is the will of God in Christ Jesus concerning you"* I Thessalonians 5:18. What does that mean? It means that every single thing that you are going through—the good, the bad, the ugly—is for the purpose of transforming your heart and bringing God's life to you on this earth. He brings His qualities and fruits into our life because we are being prepared for eternity in a place called heaven. To bring you to that place where your rewards will be piling up because God is a good God. I want to have everything that God desires to do through my life for His purpose when I get to heaven because of understanding one thing: I am not a short-term investor but a long-term investor, and I am laying up treasure in heaven, where moth and rust don't corrupt, where thieves can't break through and steal. That is where our reward is, so this world should mean nothing to us except that God's purpose would be done here on earth through us.

It is exciting to know God through His Word and to know how He wants us to respond, but I caution you at this point. Remember, the Word says (here's the important part and where Satan gets most young Christians), *"For I say through the grace given unto me that every man that is among you ought not to think of himself more highly than he ought to think, but to think soberly according as God has dealt every man the measure of faith."* The worst thing that can happen to us as a young Christian is to be lifted up in pride. James 4:6 states, *"But He giveth more grace. Wherefore He saith, God resisteth the proud, but giveth grace unto the humble."* Basically, we can say, "if you are puffed up with pride, you will be left out of the move of God." That's what Satan wants to do, and then we think we are better than everyone else and that we know everything. That's the greatest lie there ever was. I was reading the Scripture that says, *"I can do all thing through Christ who strengthens me."* Is your emphasis on the 'I' or on the 'Christ'? Unfortunately for me, it was on the 'I' for a few years. Now, the only way I can do anything is through Christ. All that I am, all that I have, exists in my realm through Christ. Without Him I have nothing, and that's kind of embarrassing, but it's the truth.

GOD CHANGES US

As we press in to know God and obey the Word, a transformation begins to happen. God changes us. 2 Corinthians 3:18 says, *"But we all, with open face beholding as in a glass the glory of the Lord, are changed into the same image from glory to glory, even as by the Spirit of the Lord."* The Bible shows us who we really are and what our life should look like. We all use a mirror to comb our hair, it shows us a reflection of how we look. We then walk away from the mirror and can't remember how to comb our hair without it, because we can't see it. It is the same way with the Word of God—it shows us who we really are and without it we forget who we really are. The association of being around people that believe in God changes us. Sometimes when I am struggling, someone will come around and say, "So brother, what'd you think about what the Lord said about this Scripture?" All of a sudden, that Scripture will minister peace and direction, and I'll have the victory again. But, if I am left alone with worldly people who don't know God, I am not going to be changed. You're changed through beholding the Lord. *"I saw the Lord, he is high and lifted up and his glory filled the temple."* Why? Because through the Word of God we can see the Lord, and the Holy Spirit within us shows us God. Then there is a revelation and an illumination within us in which we can see the Lord and we can know him and find direction.

Again, James explains the process of pressing in, to not be hearers of the Word only, but doers. In chapter 1, verse 21, he says, *"Wherefore lay apart all filthiness, and superfluities of naughtiness, and receive with meekness the engrafted word, Which is able to save your souls."* Lay aside all the corrupt and evil thoughts of the world that flow through our minds and receive with meekness the Word. With what type of an attitude do I receive the Word of God? A humble, teachable attitude, which means that I don't resist and say, "Yes, but the Word just doesn't apply in my particular situation, God just didn't address what I'm going through." We must become totally convinced that there is no truth except the Word of God. We can look at the Word and at our circumstances, and if our circumstances are different, we can know because of the Word that it's going to change. If we become convinced of our circumstances instead of the power of the Word, we'll become overwhelmed with doubt and we will sink. We have to be convinced of what God says about the Word. "It's en-grafted," which means it is planted in our soul. What happens when we plant something? It begins to grow and reproduce as long as we keep watering, fertilizing and pouring life into it. Likewise, when the Word starts to germinate and to sprout within our soul, pretty soon it starts taking over our life. What if we don't receive the Word of God? We will miss the engraft-ing process! The Word won't be implanted within us, it won't germinate in us, and we will be born-again Christians with carnal minds. Real miracle restoration revival can never take place in any country until tradition is broken down. Tradition is a belief or practice, not derived directly from the Bible, but arising and handed down within the Christian community. As long as we stay in the bondage of our natural thinking we will stay in bondage to the ways and traditions of the world. The faith that speaks and yet does not do what it is saying is really unbelief. True faith produces the fruit of good works (James 1:22-25, 2:26).

Mark 7:7-9, 13 states, *"Howbeit in vain do they worship me, teaching for doctrines the commandments of men. For laying aside the commandments of God, ye hold the tradition of men, as the washing of pots and cups; and many other such like things ye do. Full well ye reject the commandment of God, that ye may keep your own tradition.* Vs. 13, *"Making the Word of God of none effect through your traditions, which ye have delivered: and many such like."* Our traditions make the Word of God of no effect.

Fear of persecution is the main reason most Christians adhere so closely to the form, ritual, ceremony and religious tradition. We are afraid of what the people would say. Yet one can be blind to the things of God, unsaved and even demon possessed and think he is doing God a favor by speaking against you, but in reality, he is doing a work for the devil.

A Christian without the Word engrafted within him or her is like a new car with no engine. You see the car, but it doesn't run. As Christians, we have no purpose until God gets a hold of our life, then we become Spirit filled and have a purpose. The result of this is that we have a revelation of God's purpose, which transforms our lives and thinking and begins to manifest God's ways through our lives and thinking. We begin to lay hands on the sick and run to God instead of running to everyone else. We begin to live a life that's characteristic of Christ himself because it's Christ who then becomes our life.

It is God's idea that we are blameless! It is His idea that we are righteous! It is His idea we are accepted in the beloved! We are to get over ourselves and stop hindering what He says about us through His Son and get on with Him! This is the normal Christian life! The reason it's the normal Christian life is because we love our neighbors as ourselves. It is the second greatest commandment and it is tied to the first. It is like the first. So if you don't have a good opinion of yourself and if you are not free in yourself, then you don't see yourself through God's eyes. We think the Gospel is all about the fact that you and I have sinned and Jesus had to die and pay a terrible price to take away the sin, but what then? You take away the sin for what? Because we are left sinners? No! He took away the sin because there is something under the sin that is of great value worth redeeming, worth the blood of Jesus and it is called YOU and ME! We need to see ourselves in agreement with Him. The Gospel is more about our value and redeeming our value than the fact that you and I have missed the mark!

Romans 6:11 teaches this process, *"Likewise* (talking about being dead) *reckon ye also yourselves to be dead indeed unto sin, but alive unto God through Jesus Christ our Lord."* Does anybody not understand what sin is? We all fully understand that, don't we? So what do we have to do? We have to realize that that person, the old Dan, doesn't live here anymore. I was born again and the old Dan is dead; this body is dead unto the things of the world. That is reckoning ourselves dead indeed unto sin. *"But alive unto God through Jesus Christ our Lord."* Then it says, *"Let not sin therefore reign in your mortal body, that ye should obey it in the lusts thereof. Neither yield ye your members of instruments of unrighteousness unto sin. But yield yourselves unto God, as those that are alive from the dead, and your members as instruments of righteousness unto God."* So we have a choice. Man in his fallen state (before you were born again) has Satan as his lord, sin as his nature and self as his life. When we are born again, who becomes Lord? Jesus becomes Lord, righteousness becomes our nature and God becomes our life. God is asking us to walk in our new birth. How do we do that? Forget the past, forget whoever you thought you were, whatever you thought you were going to do and what you did in the past! His mercies are new every morning, thank God. Sin can't hinder you from the purpose of God because you're forgiven. God doesn't even see our sins. According to 2 Corinthians 5:17, *"All things became new."* Your past actions were done in ignorance because you did not have a revelation of Jesus Christ as Lord in your life because your mind wasn't enlightened by the Spirit of God. So repent of your sins, go forward, and be devoted to God, which will cause you to be determined to seek His purpose and walk in newness of life.

LIVING BY FAITH

We were born again by faith, but that is our first step. We have seen that our transformation to become more Christ-like and walk in the Kingdom of God as bona fide citizens takes many processes. We must renew our minds, meditate the Word, press in to know God, and allow Him to change us.

What is the common denominator for all this? Faith! Faith is truth itself; it is the proof that things which you and I may never personally verify as happened, really did happen. Hebrews ll:8, Abraham went out not knowing where he was going, he obeyed God and relied on Him to clear the path. How do we keep our faith fueled? If you remember, Jesus promised to send the Helper—the Holy Spirit.

It is important that you don't neglect the Holy Spirit. He is within you and wants to talk to you, lead you and guide you, and desires to be your life. Jude 20 instructs us to, *"Build ourselves up in the most Holy faith by praying in the spirit."* Praying in tongues is vital; pray in tongues and then listen for the Spirit because the Spirit Himself wants to direct your life. Jesus lives within us now. The apostle Paul understood it best when he said, *"It is no longer I that live but Christ that lives in me. The life I live I live by the faith of the son of God."* Not *"**a**"* faith—many new translations have changed this from "the" to "**a**" faith, but I live by "the" Faith of the Son of God. Not "**a**" faith because Christ in me produces "the" faith for God's purposes for me. There are times when I need the gift of faith because I'm wavering.

In 1978 we bought an 850-seat auditorium that had been used for mountain music concerts in Green Mountain Falls, Colorado, a town of about 600 people, to hold services for the people we had been pastoring. Many of the people thought that I was an egoist by thinking that we could have this building. I had a meeting with the members (which were about 110 people) of the church at the time before we bought it, explaining what God was asking of us and when the meeting ended we had lost about half our congregation. That first Sunday morning there were only 34 people in the new building! I had bought the building, trusting God! I was sure the building was going to be packed that first Sunday, rocking and rolling and filled to capacity, but instead we only had 34 people. I preached the message with my eyes half closed because doubt and fear were all over me, but God knew better. Over time the building filled up two times on a Sunday because of God's purpose. Every time you step out for God, Satan will do everything he can to make you look like a fool and bring discouragement, but I would rather be a fool for God anyhow. Whose fool are you?

I like to play baseball, and I could hit the ball when I was young. I always expected to hit a home-run. I wanted to hit that ball out of that park, which was my whole methodology. This is the same way I am with God: I believe I serve an awesome God, I believe He has no lack, I believe His Word is absolutely true, and I believe if He tells you to do something, do it because He will see you through. Your mind will tell you not to do it; everything in the soul realm will want you to stop—unless your mind is renewed. A renewed mind will cause you to step out in faith as you serve God. Serving God is a walk, and it is a faith walk, not a faith sit. It means becoming a doer of the Word. We do have to sit and meditate on God's Word sometimes to receive directions for our faith walk. The point to remember is that we are all important to God, but the only thing that separates us from the rest of the world is when we do what God tells us to do—when we step out in faith and serve God.

John Wesley said, "The devil has given to the church a substitute for faith, that looks and sounds so much like faith that people can't tell the difference and it's called mental ascent. It is in their head but not their hearts." They have a church experience but not a born-again experience. Faith grows out of the Word of God.

When I became a Christian, my family didn't have much to do with me for the first three years. They thought I had lost my mind. Yet, when we had the tenth anniversary celebration for the church, every relative was there—mom, dad, sister, brother, uncles, aunts, cousins—because they knew that Dan was different. Something happened to Dan because God is real.

If you have to step out and you feel like you are exposed, naked before God, that is where you need to be. You may look like you are a complete idiot to the world, but who cares? If you don't step out, you will stay in the boat and always laugh at Peter for walking on water because he started to drown. Let's be water walkers! Let's not be afraid of what the world says. Let's not be ashamed of God! Let's stand up and do the things of God! You know, in my own life, there are seasons of doing things where I am so comfortable that I wonder if I missed God. This is unfamiliar water. Usually I am on the brink of disaster, but in the middle of a miracle. I always say, "God generally terrifies you before He edifies you." We will soon discover that faith is not a work—it is a relationship built on trust with God through His Word. Everybody wants to go to heaven but very few want to know the Lord.

Fear comes when we assess our circumstances according to our mind and abilities instead of God. You may think, "Well, if I step out and it isn't God, then what?" Just remember, "If God cannot keep your boat afloat, you have no business sailing it." In other words, you will begin sinking if it isn't the right thing. I have started things that were probably my own flesh or ideas, but I soon knew it wasn't God when He did not prosper that venture. But, I was willing and obedient to step out because I didn't want to miss God. Sometimes it is difficult as Christians to clearly hear His voice and understand what He is saying.

We are convinced that God is God, but are we convinced that He is the God of the Bible and that He will do these things for us. When we started our church in Green Mountain Falls, Colorado, it was a miracle. God uses the foolish things of the world to confound the wise. After the church got going, people came and asked, "How do you do this? What are your steps to ministry? What is your vision?" I don't have a clue! I just showed up and so did He. That is how we did it! I don't know why one succeeds and someone else doesn't. And I'm not so sure that the one that doesn't isn't more important to God than the one that succeeded in the realm of the natural. It's not even about numbers; it's about the will of God, reaching people, training in discipleship and being open to be a vessel of God; and walking in the Spirit and bringing love, acceptance and forgiveness to a hurting world.

STEPPING OUT IN FAITH

We were in a Full Gospel Businessmen's Meeting, newly saved and sitting in the front row (the best place to sit since there are no distractions, but the downside is you don't know who is sitting behind you). There we were in this meeting, born again Christians, baptized in the Holy Spirit, and the teacher says, "Okay turn around and pray for the people behind you." I turn around and there is a lady in a wheelchair. I'm thinking "Whoops! This is not for me maybe there is someone else here to pray for." See, I was moved by sight, not faith. And then the man said again, "Turn around and pray for that lady." I looked at him and I am thinking, "You man of faith and power, why don't you come and pray for her?" All I could think of is that someone else needed to pray for her, but we turned around and prayed, and the lady got healed and got up out of her wheelchair. I thought, "How in the world did that happen?" During most of my ministry when I have seen healings, I have still been shocked by them and I can't figure out how they happened. I found out that the only way healing works is for us to do what the Word says and I have learned to trust God for the results.

With God, you can be in the marketplace and He will say something to you about praying for somebody else. And you think, "Oh no, here we go again," and then you are obedient to His leading. Or, you know you are supposed to share that reality with somebody, and everybody knows we don't want to share Christ with anybody. I mean, unfortunately that is what happens because the world is so against Jesus, isn't it?

But, you know what? All you have to do is say, "What are your Spiritual beliefs?" Be really interested and get them talking first. Then they will say, "Well, what do you think?" And you respond, "Well, you know . . ." Then you mention the name of Jesus and the Holy Spirit takes over.

We need to understand that there are two parts at play in everything you receive from God. The part that the Lord plays and the part you play. God will never fail in doing His part! And if you do your part, you can be sure of victory.

FAITH WALK – NOT FAITH SIT

Hebrews Chapter 11:1 tells us that, "Faith (truth itself) is the substance (the foundation) of things hoped (expected, to look forward with conviction) for, the evidence of things not seen." Faith originates in God's Word, and is directly related to God's Word. Faith is knowing something is true. The one point we have to realize is that faith confesses that unseen things are real because we learn to walk with God and see things as He sees them. Faith is not just understanding the Word of God, faith is believing it and living by it. Now verse 8 says, *"By faith, Abraham, when he was called to go out into a place which he should after receive for an inheritance, obeyed; and he went out, not knowing where he was going."* Where did this come from? Well if you go back to John 3:8, it says that the Holy Spirit comes upon us and it's like a wind. You don't know where it has been, and you don't know where it is going. So, if you're ready for a faith-filled life, you had better get ready to start living not knowing where you are going because that is exactly what the Holy Spirit does. It blows you from one point of existence to another for the purpose of God and you just have to be willing to go. Just like the nation of Israel, crossing through the wilderness, they didn't know what was going to happen the next day. The Spirit, the cloud, the fire, may begin moving again and they had to get ready to follow it. You live so intent with God today, desiring that His will be done and you just know that tomorrow is going to take care of itself. God has already promised you that. But, Hebrews Chapter 11:1 says, *"Now, faith is the substance of things hoped for. The evidence of things not seen."* Faith begins with your hope in what God's Word says, knowing that you are more than a conqueror through Christ. Regardless of the situation you're in, you are going to stand your ground and see the salvation of the Lord. True faith is not based on empirical evidence but on divine God-given present assurance of a future reality. Faith is the opposite of the law, and the more people become self-conscious and the more we look at our self efforts to receive from the Lord, the less faith we will have in the Lord.

"Faith moves and acts as God moves and acts. Reason is troubled, excited, and nervous; faith stands unmoved. Faith knows that God cannot lie, so faith never argues, but takes it for granted when a request has been made according to the word of God. Faith considers a work as finished, even before it is manifested.

Faith does not consider what the natural eye can see, what the natural ear can hear, or what the physical body can feel. Faith heeds only God's promise."

–T.L. Osborn.

Faith for any breakthrough or miracle in your life springs forth when you see His grace. Most of us only see our works, unrighteousness, and failures and are not "Looking unto Jesus the author and finisher of our faith". I believe with all my heart as we come under grace and are delivered from the works of the law, faith will no longer be a struggle or barrier because we will walk with unconscious faith. In the past we put our faith in our own faith and it didn't work. We need to put our faith in God's grace and love for us. The Bible says that "Faith works by love" not our love for God but God's love for us. Stop wondering if you have enough faith and just believe that it is His blood alone that saves, delivers and blesses us!

Verse 11:8 tells us that Abraham took off without knowing where he was going. Let me tell you something about serving God: you do not know where you are going. I have been all over the world and in places I would have never believed. I have seen things that are just beyond anything I thought I would ever see. I never, at any point, imagined that I could live the life that I have lived. I have a friend who said, "You are kind of like the 'CIA' aren't you?" I said, "Yes, Christians in Action." Because there are times when the Holy Spirit will put a country on my heart, and in a couple of weeks I will be there. Going into Cuba for four years, where we had sixteen National Pastor and Leadership Conferences has been really exciting, and we were able to smuggle a lot of Christian material to the people there—we filled our biggest suitcases.

At the Havana airport, dogs sniff out the suitcases, and one was hanging around my suitcase and just getting ready to sit down when its handler called it to quit because it was lunchtime. Thank you, Jesus! The one mistake I made when being interrogated was on my first trip into Cuba when they asked me what type of a Christian I was, and I froze and said, "Protestant!" They said, "You are a protestor?" I should have said, "Evangelical." I was then able to tell them I was with a denomination, and they allowed me right in. Many of the officials are Christians.

A friend of mine went into China with a lot of Christian materials. At customs, they started questioning him about what he was doing there. He started speaking in tongues, and you know what? They couldn't find an interpreter, and they let him through because they didn't understand the language he was speaking. Another brother in Christ was put in jail in Cuba for three months just for doing the very same things I do. He started to preach from his Bible in prison and wanted to see the captain, so they took him to see the captain. He threw his Bible down on the captain's desk. At this point, it is important to note that they call us spies down there. My friend asked, "How many spies carry Bibles around that are this well worn? How many spies can preach the gospel like I can preach the gospel?" The captain looked at him because many of them are Christian, and they let him out. Why was he in there three months? I can put it simply: he has a testimony, and if you look closely at the first four letters of that word—TEST—you will understand, and everything he or you or I are going through is preparation for heaven. This world is temporal. It isn't about how much money you can make. It is about the will of God being fulfilled in your life. That is why you start meditating the Word of God; you meditate it night and day. You begin to know the language of the Kingdom of God and the ways of God. You begin to understand that what God said is true, and that no matter what you are going through because the Word is true.

I was on an airplane where the ride was so rough people were being thrown all around inside, and were yelling fearfully. Later, I found out we were flying through a hurricane on our way to Cuba from Panama. I punched a friend of mine and said, "What is the Spanish word for 'help'?" and he laughed. Sometimes, humor keeps us from crying. In your heart you know you are okay, and this is not the way you are going to die. God is going to bring you through, but the devil will do everything in the world to try to destroy those things around you to try and get you to focus on them instead of deliverance. But, once you focus on deliverance, you see the salvation of the Lord all the time. What you are focusing on, you will see. It's the enemy who tries to get us to think that the Christian walk is like the 100-yard dash. It's actually a 26-mile marathon, and you have just begun. It's progressive and will take the rest of your life, and as you begin to overcome, you become stronger and stronger and stronger so that all hell couldn't tear you away from your purpose because *"Greater is He that is in you than He that is in the world."*

In Hebrews Chapter 11:9 it says, *"By faith he sojourned in the land of promise, as in a strange country, dwelling in tabernacles with Isaac and Jacob, the heir with him of the same promise."* We find in the Old Testament that they sojourned in the land of promise. Let me tell you the difference between the Old Testament and the New Testament. In the Old Testament, Abraham's blessing was the land of Israel; in the New Testament, the blessing is the life of God according to John 10:10. Jesus speaks, *"I have come to give you life and life more abundantly,"* and that life is the *"Zóé"* life of God. You contend for the life of God within you from the point of having the blessing—you are "already blessed." You begin your journey as a Christian pursuing the life that God has for you.

Abraham looked for a land, a city that had foundations and whose builder and maker was God. Hebrews 11:11, *"Through faith also Sarah herself received strength to conceive seed, and was delivered of a child when she was past age, because she judged him faithful who had promised."* Where do you begin? You begin by taking the Word of God as absolute truth. Every single word is true. When God starts to speak to you, He is faithful. Verse 12, *"Therefore sprang there even of one, and him as good as dead, so many as the stars of the sky in multitude, and as the sand which is by the sea shore innumerable."* All these children that were brought forth died in faith. Verse 13 says, *"These all died in faith, not having received the promises, but having seen them afar off, and were persuaded of them, and embraced them and confessed that they were strangers and pilgrims on the earth."* It is interesting that they saw the promise afar off. This is how it was with me at first. I saw the promise of God as some distant thing, but now that I have pursued it, now that I have pressed in, the present reality is that in all things I am more than a conqueror. And then it goes on to say, *"and were persuaded of them."* As we grow in grace, we are enabled by the Spirit to believe God's promises and we become persuaded of them. How do they persuade us? You lay hands on the sick, you pray for those that need to be saved, you lead people in the baptism of the Holy Spirit, you pray in the spirit, you allow your faith to grow and you become persuaded by the answers to your prayers.

It took me many months of study to be convinced of the baptism of the Holy Spirit and then once I was persuaded of it, I realized it was the language of men and of angels. This is the language that I will have in heaven. When I speak through the Spirit I know that I am "speaking out" the will of God for my life. I am confessing it in the Spirit. How powerful it is when we pray in the Spirit! And then it says, *"They embraced this promise."* We clutch to ourselves the promises of God. We become so convinced of this that there is no way anybody anywhere can ever talk us out of them. There is no other purpose that you will ever live your life for besides the will and purpose of God. You are embracing God's promises and only then can we go to the next stage.

Finally, we confess, according to Hebrews 11:3, *"That we are strangers and pilgrims on this earth."* We become strangers to our old way of life, and Matthew 16:24 must become our confession and lifestyle. *"Then Jesus said to His disciples, If anyone desires to come after Me, let him deny himself, and take up his cross, and follow Me."* We have chosen a new country that has new laws and a new language. We must put our trust in God, even when circumstances don't look promising. We choose to live a surrendered life to him.

"Now faith is the substance of things hoped for, the evidence of things not seen."

-Hebrews 11:1

When you hope for something, where does it exist? Only in your mind and in your heart. It is only a possibility. What makes it appear? You, the believer, with faith that gives substance to your hopes and dreams. Faith sees that which is not and gives it substance so that it may appear and become visible. Your expectations and beliefs are of primary importance. If you observe and expect failure, sickness or disaster, that is exactly what will manifest. There are an infinite number of possibilities that exist for your life. You alone have the power to choose which possibility becomes reality. Choose wisely.

– Adapted from Annette Capps, "Quantum Faith"

CHAPTER 5

OUR COMMISSION TO PREACH THE KINGDOM OF GOD

Each one of us has an active role in the Kingdom of God, and we have the Word of God to guide us. God has commanded us to do certain things as citizens of His Kingdom. For example, being obedient and understanding the supernatural law of sowing and reaping are some of these principles.

Jesus spoke the following Scriptures to the disciples telling them what they were to do.

> Matthew 28:18-20, *"And Jesus came and spake unto them, saying all power is given unto me in heaven and earth. Go ye therefore, and teach all nations, baptizing them in the name of the Father, and of the Son, and of the Holy Spirit: teaching them to observe all things whatsoever I have commanded you: and, lo, I am with you always, even unto the end of the world."*

> Mark 16:15-20, *"And He said unto them, Go ye into all the world, and preach the gospel to every creature. He that believeth and is baptized shall be saved; but he that believeth not shall be damned. And these signs shall follow them that believe; In my name shall they cast out devils; they shall speak with new tongues; they shall take up serpents; and if they drink any deadly thing, it shall not hurt them; they shall lay hands on the sick, and they shall recover. So then after the Lord had spoken unto them, He was received up into heaven, and sat on the right hand of God. And they went forth, and preached every where, the Lord working with them and confirming the word with signs following."*

John the Baptist preached for the people to repent, for the Kingdom of God was at hand. Jesus came preaching the Kingdom, and He also told his disciples to preach the Kingdom of God. In His last forty days on the earth, Jesus was teaching and preaching the things pertaining to the Kingdom of God (Acts 1:3). Later, in Acts 28, the apostle Paul was teaching the things pertaining to the Kingdom of God.

Romans 14:17 identifies the Kingdom of God for us: *"For the Kingdom of God is not meat nor drink, but it is righteousness, and peace and joy in the Holy Spirit."* God's intention from the beginning was that He would have a nation of people who are walking in the Holy Spirit, with righteousness, peace and joy as a kingdom of priests. Until we understand the truth of the kingdom of priests and the priesthood, we will never walk in righteousness, peace and joy.

OBEDIENCE VERSUS REBELLION IN THE KINGDOM OF GOD

Let's look at Jeremiah 5:20-25 which begins, *"Declare this in the house of Jacob, and publish it in Judah, saying, Hear now this, o foolish people, and without understanding; which have eyes and see not; which have ears, and hear not?"* When God speaks to the nation of Israel in the New Testament, He is talking about these same people. They have eyes, but they see not; they have ears, but they hear not. Verse 22 continues, *"Fear ye not me?"* He is saying, "Don't you reverence me? Don't you believe me?" *"Saith the Lord: will ye not tremble at my presence, which have placed the sand for the bound of the sea by a perpetual decree, that it cannot pass it: and though the waves thereof toss themselves, yet can they not prevail; though they roar, yet can they not pass over it? But this people,"*—the Jews— *"hath a revolting and a rebellious heart; they are revolted and gone."* God is saying to them, "You don't respect me enough to believe me. I am the one who set the boundaries of the oceans, the waves come in but they cannot go past my boundaries. You have revolted against me. You are rebellious; you have taken and gone away to do your own will. You are exalting your knowledge, ideas, and will above me." Verse 24, *"Neither say they in their heart, let us now fear the Lord our God, that giveth rain, both the former and the latter, in his season: he reserveth unto us the appointed weeks of the harvest."* Verse 25, *"Your iniquities have turned away these things, and your sins have withholden good things from you."* God is talking to this nation of people, saying that they are the ones who are rebelling against Him. Their sins have turned away good things. He came to give life and life more abundantly. He hasn't changed. He wants to give us a life that is producing righteousness, peace and joy in our hearts, but someplace along the line, we are going to have to lay down our natural wisdom and accept His supernatural guidance through the Holy Spirit. Israel would not do that. They refused to let God lead and guide them into their promised land. In Deuteronomy 30:19 it states, "I call heaven and earth to record this day against you, that I have set before you life and death, blessings and cursing: therefore choose life, that both thou and thy seed may live;" God is still giving us the choice to serve Him in accordance to His Word or continue living in the flesh and being overcome. When this happens, there is another principle that is working in the earth: the principle of sowing and reaping.

The devil wants us to be bound up in sin. It is only when God's Word becomes alive in us that we can be set free. When we sin, we open up avenues for the devil to get into our lives. This is the principle given to us in Galatians 6:7-8, the laws of sowing and reaping. If you are tired of being defeated it is time to pick up your scepter of righteousness and shake it in the devil's face. It is time to kick sin out of our lives and start living free.

SOWING AND REAPING

Galatians 6:7-9 says, *"What we sow is what we reap."* Now the good news is that we can apply the positive to that and say, "God, I am going to sow good things, and I don't care what it looks like. I am going to sow good things because I will also reap if I faint not."

It is not God, if we have chosen the wrong path. The reason we reap what we sow is because we get out of God's will and move into the devil's, and it is then we reap corruption because we sow unto the flesh (Galatians 6:8). The devil understands the laws of sowing and reaping, and we need to understand them, too. It is because of this principle that we don't always understand what is going on in the lives of others. This is the job for the Righteous Judge: the Lord Himself will judge this matter righteously and will bless us as we bless His seed.

The words "faint not" mean that we are going to have to exercise patience in times of adversity. The enemy will do everything he can to keep us in the bondage of fear and lack, which causes us to want to act out of the flesh and make things happen ahead of God, just like Abraham and Ishmael did. We constantly must realize that God has everything under control, and all is in His timing not ours. It seems God will miss a hundred opportunities to be early, but He is always on time. We must remember our walk is an eternal walk, and we must think in terms of eternity to understand that *"everything is working to our good."* When we lengthen our time span and start thinking of things in terms of eternal time spans, it is then that we will be set free to trust God no matter what! It is only when we want God to do something today that we get into trouble. God has been around forever, He is going to be here forever and He is in absolutely no hurry for anybody. There is an old saying, "Our lack of planning (faith) does not create an emergency for Him."

In the story of Mary and Martha (John 11), their brother Lazarus was dying, and they ran to Jesus and said that Lazarus was dying. Jesus continued to do what He was doing and did not go immediately to Lazarus. A couple of days had passed, and He finally went to them and Lazarus was dead. Jesus was not worried because he knew the power of God in His life. Jesus raised Lazarus from the dead, and He did the will of God in God's timing. I am sure Mary and Martha were having a very difficult time believing that Jesus was acting in their best interest. Was not Jesus supposed to be their friend, had they not done things for Him, did He not care? They needed to rest in the fact that Jesus had everything under control. Jesus did not have to act in the natural when He knew the supernatural. That is why we will reap if we faint not. God's timing is for our best interest. God desires to transform us into the image of His dear Son. We need to exercise our faith in God and trust Him no matter what. We must stop acting in the flesh with our natural minds and senses and believe God, and then His blessing will come upon us!

Psalm 78:32-42 tells us that even after God performed many miracles, *"For all this they sinned still."* He worked miraculously in their lives, He demonstrated Himself as God, and they believed not His wonderful works. Verse 33, *"Therefore, their days did he consume in vanity, and their years in trouble."* Because they rejected God, they spent their lives in vanity, which produced fear. *"When He slew them, then they sought him: and they returned and inquired early after God."* He certainly knows how to get our attention! *"And they remembered that God was their rock, and the high God their redeemer. Nevertheless they did flatter him with their mouth, and they lied unto him with their tongues. For their heart was not right with him, neither were they steadfast in His covenant."* God's covenant is solid, steadfast and unmovable, but it is our reaction to it that causes His response, or lack of response, in our lives. It is what is in our heart that produces the fruit of it. *"But He, being full of compassion, forgave their iniquity, and destroyed them not: yea, many a time turned he his anger away, and did not stir up all His wrath. For he remembered that they were but flesh; a wind that passeth away, and cometh not again. How often did they provoke Him in the wilderness, and grieve Him in the desert. Yea, they turned back and tempted God, and limited the Holy One of Israel. They remembered not his hand, nor the day when he delivered them from the enemy."*

Proverbs 20:21 says, *"Man's goings are of the Lord, how can a man understand then his way."* This is where faith comes in because man's goings are like the wind, according to John 3:8. God has placed us on this earth for His purpose. Our goings are of the Lord and are for His divine design and eternal purposes. The nation of Israel fought this, and turned their back on God. They turned back, they tempted God and they limited God. I believe today our churches are full of people, sometimes including the leadership, who have turned away from the leadership of the Holy Spirit and are limiting God's will in the earth today. You can ask them, "Who is Lord?" and they will confess Jesus as Lord, but the fruit of Jesus' lordship is not seen in their lives. Jesus wants to live through our lives and, in exchange, He will give you eternal life as well as an abundant life here on this earth and in the world to come. Many want the reward of obedience, but in return do not want to be obedient. Too many want to use God, but do not want to be used of God. There is a big difference.

The Kingdom of God is truly just that! We belong to God, and we are no longer our own; our lives are to be used to glorify God and to do His will. We are all ambassadors of the King. In the devil's kingdom nobody is an ambassador for anyone, it's everybody for themselves. They all have their own perverse agenda and only represent themselves. This was Satan's original sin: he wanted to represent himself and do his will rather than God's. Jesus came to only do what the Father told Him, and that is the difference. Satan did his own will, and Jesus only did God's will and did not speak on His own account. Satan came to only do his own thing. Nobody's going to tell him what to do.

Many today are espousing the grace message. Grace came to teach the child of God to stand against sin and flee from it, not to ignore it. Grace is for the living, not the dead! I believe in it, however, it was not given unto us to continue in sin, God forbid! Proverbs 28:13 says, *"He that covers his sin shall not prosper."* When we continue in sin, God is saying that we will not prosper in the things of God. A sure way not to prosper is to continue in sin. Will God forgive sin if we repent? Yes, He will! But, if we continue to sin it will bring lack into our lives. God forgives, but the devil never forgets. The more we sin willfully, the more our hearts will be hardened against God. When your heart is hardened against God, you will not hear His voice. You will hear only the voice of the enemy, which brings self-justification into our lives. You will have so limited God that you will frustrate His grace, and He will not be able to bless you. Because God is no respecter of persons, He gives us all the same map—the Word of God that says to us, "Go and tell" and "Go and do," but most of us sit and stew. Why? Because we didn't go and do. This world is so temporary, but our map—the Word of God—gives us specifics on how to live, and it is eternal. Even in these verses, God gives us clear instructions for what we are to do:

Colossians 3:1, *"If ye then be risen with Christ, seek those things which are above, where Christ sitteth on the right hand of God. Set your affections on things above, not on things on the earth."*

Proverbs 3:4-5, *"Trust in the Lord with all your heart and lean not unto thine own understanding. In all your ways acknowledge him, and He shall direct your paths."*

Psalm 37:23, *"The steps of a good man are ordered of the Lord. Though he fall down, he shall not be utterly cast down: for the Lord upholdeth him with His hand."* Why do we fall? Because our ways are of the Lord, and we don't understand His will because we haven't meditated His Word. Though we fall, we need to get back up and keep going. God doesn't utterly reject us when we sin. We utterly reject God when we lean unto our own understanding, when we exalt ourselves.

Mark 16:15-20, *"And He said unto them, Go ye into all the world, and preach the gospel to every creature. He that believeth and is baptized shall be saved; but he that believeth not shall be damned. And these signs shall follow them that believe; In my name shall they cast out devils; they shall speak with new tongues; they shall take up serpents; and if they drink any deadly thing, it shall not hurt them; they shall lay hands on the sick, and they shall recover. So then after the Lord had spoken unto them, He was received up into heaven, and sat on the right hand of God. And they went forth, and preached every where, the Lord working with them and confirming the word with signs following."* Again, God takes us from something to nothing for the purpose of His creative ability.

It's not about our comfort, but about His will. When we are obedient to His Word and go and preach the gospel, it is then His responsibility to confirm the gospel to those who hear it. However, we won't see the life-changing power of the gospel save the lost and usher them into the Kingdom of God until we "go and do." We can sit at home and believe God all we want, but until we obey the Word—until we "go and do"—nothing we do on our own will bring us true peace because we are anointed for His purpose, not ours. God's provision is in the place God has called us to. However, "following His purpose" comes through faith, yet we think it is easier to live our own life (in the flesh) and live a comfortable life doing our own temporal thing, but that results in no eternal purpose. Failure is being successful at something that really doesn't matter eternally.

Our response to God should be, "Father, send me. Whatever your creative purpose in my life is, Father, let your will be done! I don't have to go and bury the dead (Matthew 8:22). I don't have to go and do this or that. Lord, I am ready to go now!" It is when we are helpless in the natural that we will see God's strength in the supernatural. Just don't get confused and think it was you, lest you get into pride and the scripture tells us, *"A man's pride shall bring him low: but honour shall uphold the humble in spirit"* (Proverbs 29:23).

God took the Kingdom of God away from Israel and gave it unto us because of their unbelief. They limited Him; they didn't believe Him. Hebrews 4:2, *"For unto us was the gospel preached, as well as unto them: but the word preached did not profit them, not being mixed with faith in them that heard it."* They didn't mix the Word with faith. From the foundations of the world, each generation has had its own opportunity to lay up treasure in heaven by responding to the will of God. It is now our time and turn. The problem we run into is that we desire the things of the world in our own way and time more than we desire the things of God. What He wants us to do is set our affections upon things that are above, upon the Kingdom of God. He wants us in His Kingdom, walking within His boundaries, tending to His business, working within His timeframe, and enjoying His provision. Check your location and your priorities. Are you pressing into the Kingdom of God? If God is speaking to you today, what is your response?

CHAPTER 6

GOD'S COVENANT

In the last chapter, we learned that God wants us to understand His Kingdom, walking within His boundaries, tending to His business, working within His timeframe, and enjoying His provision to do it. He guides us in this through His Word, and our right response is obedience. But, we are not merely following directions; we have a divine covenant with the Almighty King and Creator of the Universe!

Looking at 1 Peter 2:9-12 again, *"But you are a chosen generation, a royal priesthood, a holy nation, a peculiar people; that ye should show forth the praises of Him who hath called you out of darkness into His marvelous light: which in times past were not a people but are now the people of God: which had not obtained mercy, but now have obtained mercy. Dearly beloved, I beseech you as strangers and pilgrims, abstain from fleshly lusts, which war against the soul; Having your conversation honest among the Gentiles; that, whereas they speak against you as evildoers, they may by your good works, which they shall behold, glorify God in the day of visitation."* I was totally frustrated for about six months over this verse. I couldn't get revelation knowledge of how this was to be in my life as a doer, not just a knower. Through studying other saints' understanding on this, I began to grasp how this was to be affected into my life. Let us go back to the Old Testament, and start where God begins in the revelation of His Kingdom.

Exodus 19:5, *"Now, therefore, if ye will obey my voice indeed, and keep my covenant, then ye shall be a peculiar treasure unto me a kingdom of priests, and a holy nation. These are the words (Moses), which thou shalt speak unto the children of Israel."* Since the very beginning, God has had a plan for every believer in every generation. From the beginning He has had a plan, even for us today, because of who He is. He tells us, "I am the Lord, I do not change."

God is looking for those who will respond to and follow the Word of God. Unfortunately, what we see as we follow history is that time and time again, people—God's people—come to Him, and then are drawn away by the lusts of this world and by the prince of darkness, who has come to deceive the children of God and entangle (Galatians 5:1) them again in the ways of this world. When we follow what Jesus taught, we will conform to Biblical principles, turn from our own wicked ways, and live a crucified life. We either will serve God or mammon, according to Matthew 6:24, *"No man can serve two masters: for either he will hate the one and love the other; or else he will hold to the one, and despise the other. Ye cannot serve God and mammon."*

Romans 14:17, *"The Kingdom of God is not meat nor drink but it is righteousness, peace and joy in the Holy Spirit."* We sometimes believe that God just doesn't really understand what it is like to live on this earth. We question His wisdom and exalt our knowledge, end up in deception, and then blame God for our problems. Yet, the Bible says He was tempted in all points. So, God does know, He does understand the time we are living in, and He does have a plan for us in this generation. The good news is that, *"Jesus Christ is the same yesterday, and today, and forever"* (Hebrews 13:8), and *"There is nothing new under the sun, all is vanity"* (Ecclesiastes 1:9 and 14). Also, *"There is no temptation taken you but such as is common to man"* (1 Corinthians 10:13). All of us can sin, and everything is common. You are not going through anything that the rest of us haven't gone through, or will be going through, because there are only certain basic areas of sin. So what He is telling us is that we are a chosen generation. We are part of God's plan in this generation, according to Genesis 17:7, *"And I will establish my covenant between me and thee and thy seed after thee in their generations for an everlasting covenant, to be a God unto thee, and to thy seed after thee."* God has made an everlasting covenant with our forefathers to be a God unto all generations if we respond to Him and His Word. We are to be a holy nation, a peculiar people.

The church today is that holy nation because God said in Matthew 21 that He was going to take away the Kingdom of God from them (Israel) and give it to a nation that would bear forth its fruit, which we are. Colossians 1:13 says, *"Who hath delivered us from the power of darkness, and hath translated us into the kingdom of His dear son."* When we were born again, Christ came into our lives for the purpose of delivering us from ourselves *"and the sins that so easily beset us"* (Hebrews 12:1) so that He could become Lord in our lives. When we became born again, we became new creations, led by the Holy Spirit. The power that led us as sinners was Satan, who led us in the opposite direction of God through temptation and our ignorance of the Word of God. But, God delivered us from the power of darkness; Satan's power was broken over us (his ability to control our lives was broken). Luke 10:17-19 says, *"And the seventy returned again with joy, saying, Lord, even the devils are subject unto us through thy name. And he said unto them, I beheld Satan as lightning fall from heaven. Behold, I give unto you power to tread on serpents and scorpions, and over all the power of the enemy: and nothing shall by any means hurt you."* According to this Scripture, we have power over the enemy. We were translated into the Kingdom of God's dear Son. What is that kingdom? As I shared in Chapter 1, God's original plan from the very beginnings of this earth was a theocracy. A theocracy is a group of people who are submitted one to another in love as a chosen generation, as a royal priesthood, as a holy nation who are pursuing the Lordship of Jesus Christ.

BEING LED BY THE SPIRIT

God wants to lead our lives through the Holy Spirit into the abundant life that John 10:10 proclaims. God uses the ministry gifts to point us unto the Cross and encourage us in the right direction. His ultimate intention is that we look to Him through the Holy Spirit for direction and purpose. We are so easily drawn to men for direction that we don't want to personally press in to hear from God, but He wants us to be followers of Christ, not man!

We are a little like the nation of Israel who wanted a strong leader to guide them rather than the Spirit of God, and so they settled for Saul instead of God. Let's not fall into the same temptation! Our purpose on God's earth will only be fulfilled if we allow the Spirit of God to lead us and we respond to the personal relationship we have with Him.

II Timothy 4:16-17 says, *"At my first answer no man stood with me, but all men forsook me: I pray God that it may not be laid to their charge. Notwithstanding the Lord stood with me, and strengthened me; that by me the preaching might be fully known, and that all the Gentiles might hear: and I was delivered out of the mouth of the lion."* Paul did not allow others to keep him from God's purpose, he had to stand alone. He knew that God was standing with him and that was all he needed. It is the same in our lives; no matter who thought we had lost our way; we knew that God knew our way and would guide us. In Hebrews 11:13 it says, *"These all died in faith, not having received the promises, but having seen them afar off, were persuaded of them, and embraced them, and confessed that they were strangers and pilgrims on the earth."* Because of this, our natural mind finds it extremely difficult to understand God's ways and many do not understand. Even our families didn't understand what we were doing, where we were going, or the strange things going on in our lives. Thus, many times we have to stand alone in what we believe and just follow God.

Matthew 6:33 states, *"But seek ye first the Kingdom of God, and His righteousness: and all these things shall be added unto you."* It is when we are doing what God has called us to do that we lack nothing! God's provision is in His place of purpose, not in what we want to do. Wherever God guides, He provides. He does it through people that are hearing what He is saying to the church today. All I can tell you is that when I am moving in God, I don't have a need. When God wanted to lead us from one place to another, our provision would dry up and we would be forced to make a decision about going somewhere else.

When we were in Arkansas, we had rented a home for one month and our provision had dried up and we had to move out. The day before we were to move, God spoke to a couple sitting in front of us at church, and they asked if we needed a place to stay. They offered us a small apartment in the warehouse of the moving company they owned and moved us in rent-free until God showed us our next step.

Another financial provision came through someone that I had led to the Lord. At the motel we owned, I had the opportunity to witness to a man whose marriage was in trouble. About two months later, the man returned with his wife to stay in our motel. They wanted to go to church with Penny and me, and then to lunch to share the good news about their restored marriage. Before they left, the man asked me if I needed any money, what amount would it be? Penny and I did need $1000 at that time, but I didn't want to tell him. Well, as it turned out, he already had heard from God. He had an envelope with $1000 cash in his coat pocket, which he handed to me. What a miraculous God we serve! God met our need through someone who knew nothing about what was happening in our lives.

Another instance of God moving in a miraculous way is our testimony of how God got us from Arkansas to Colorado. The man I was working with at the time had a vision from God that Penny and I would be in Colorado within two weeks. He had also decided to move the business to Colorado. He then invited us to move with the company and allowed the same moving truck to carry all of our belongings. That was a miracle because we had no money to move. Yet, once we arrived in Colorado, God worked through many circumstances to get us to our destination, which was Woodland Park. Within nine months of being in Colorado, we were starting a church and our needs were always being met.

At other times God has provided miraculously, such as the day that I had only $9 left to my name and needed a miracle quickly. Within two days, I received $10 and $800 through unexpected sources. Penny and I have seen many miracles of provision throughout our walk with the Lord, whether it was monetary, needing a place to live, or clothing. God says that these things are added unto you. This means God will lead us to our place of provision and give us the opportunity to be blessed. We are to seek the Kingdom of God and then these things are a byproduct of seeking His purpose for our lives.

Many times provision came when people invited us to dinner and further blessed us with bags of frozen or canned food. God used so many different people in our lives, and we are thankful for the body of Christ and their obedience to hearing God's voice.

Too many people just want to sit and not do anything, expecting God to drop things out of heaven into their laps. However, I have discovered there is most always two parts at play when it comes to receiving from God. We have a part to play in obedience and if we do our part, then we can be assured that God will never fail in doing His part. Faith always demands our response!

In Mark 10:49-52, *"And Jesus stood still, and commanded him to be called. And they call the blind man, saying unto him, Be of good comfort, rise; he calleth thee. And he, casting away his garment, rose, and came to Jesus. And Jesus answered and said unto him, What wilt thou that I should do unto thee? The blind man said unto him, Lord, that I might receive my sight. And Jesus said unto him, Go thy way; thy faith hath made thee whole. And immediately he received his sight, and followed Jesus in the way."* The blind man's part was to obey Jesus and rise. He acted on Jesus' Word and received his blessings.

We know firsthand that God's covenant is a divine promise of provision. We have entered into it, lived it, had every need met, and reaped unimaginable blessings from it. Unlike the temptations of the enemy, the quick fixes of man, and shortcuts of life, God's reward for covenant living—for following Jesus' example—is beyond what we can imagine. He loves us dearly, He knows our needs, He knows the desires of our hearts, and He wants to bless us abundantly. Living in the Kingdom of God is covenant living.

CHAPTER 7

SPIRITUAL WARFARE

Much is being taught today about spiritual warfare. I believe that this is a wonderful topic to understand and to teach. However, just like other areas of our Christian walk, we seem to have run into a ditch regarding this subject. It is time we as believers gain a proper perspective of our authority. It is in understanding the full extent of the spiritual warfare raging around us we will begin to understand our part in the warfare. You can ask any Christian and they will tell you yes, they have read the Bible. Yet, it seems they do not understand that God has given us the Bible so we can walk through life on His promises. He has given us thousands of promises, and yet many people have applied none, except possibly John 3:16, to their lives.

God has given us His Word to believe and act upon so that we may have the abundant life that Jesus has come to bring us. Jesus has done His part, and now it is time that we do ours. He has called us to have faith in His

Word, so we can walk with assurance knowing we can rise above the circumstances we face. It is by standing and confessing the Word of God in the midst of our trials and temptations that we find our victory.

God has set forth in His Word certain principals and truths concerning our attitudes, thoughts and confession that will produce within us the emotional stability and peace which will cause us to have victory in our day-by-day walk with Him.

2 Corinthians 10:3-5 says, *"For though we walk in the flesh, we do not war after the flesh: (For the weapons of our warfare are not carnal, but mighty through God to the pulling down of strong holds;) Casting down imaginations, and every high thing that exalteth itself against the knowledge of God, and bringing into captivity every thought to the obedience of Christ."* We have seen that first we have a thought and if we incorporate that thought into our thinking process, we then begin to imagine and picture that thought. If we continue to meditate upon that picture, it will become a stronghold and end up controlling us. This is seen every day by the advertisements on our televisions. The advertisers want to make something so appealing, you will have to go out and buy it. It is the same with the devil—he does his best to make us think that unrighteousness is so appealing.

Proverbs 23:7 illustrates this, *"For as he thinks in his heart, so is he."* We are what we think and believe about our circumstances and ourselves in our daily lives. Most people are defeated before they even start because they don't think they can overcome the obstacles of life and they just give up hope. It is only when we confess the Word of God into our circumstances with faith and conviction, while believing in our hearts, that we rise above the fears that come our way. If our minds are not renewed, we will speak forth our fears and failures; but, if we have renewed our minds we will speak forth God's Word into our circumstances. Matthew 12:34, *"For out of the abundance of the heart the mouth speaks."*

The Christian life is not one that is free from trials and temptations; rather, it is one in which we learn to endure and overcome the obstacles of life through developing the right attitude. When we see the promises of God's Word and confess that Word with faith, we will see the victory. As Mark 9:23 says, *"If thou canst believe, all things are possible to him that believeth."* Belief is not just an idea a person possesses, belief is an idea that possesses a person.

God has given us His authority through the great commission of Jesus Christ. In Luke 10:19, Jesus tells us, *"I have given you power to tread on serpents and scorpions, and over all the power of the enemy, and nothing shall by any means hurt you."* In Matthew 28:18-19, Jesus says, *"All power is given unto me, in heaven and in earth. Go ye therefore."* He has given us authority in His name, the name of Jesus Christ.

1 Peter 5:8-9 says, *"Be sober, be vigilant; because your adversary the devil, as a roaring lion, walketh about, seeking whom he may devour."* "Whom he may" implies that we grant permission to allow the devil to devour us. It is our responsibility to be vigilant. Also, we are told to be strong in the Lord and in His power in Ephesians 6:10: *"Finally, my brethren, be strong in the Lord, and in the power of His might."* We are to act on what the Word is telling us. Why? Because 1 John 4:4 says, *"Greater is he that is in you then he that is in the world."* So our responsibility in spiritual warfare is found in Hebrews 10:23, *"Let us hold fast the profession* (or confession) *of our faith without wavering; for He is faithful that promised!"*

Satan operates in the area of suggestion, and we either reject or accept his thoughts. When we accept a thought, we actually "buy" responsibility for the thought and become guilty for the thought as Matthew 5:27-28 tells us, *"Ye have heard that it was said by them of old time, Thou shalt not commit adultery: But I say unto you, That whosoever looketh on a woman to lust after her hath committed adultery with her already in his heart."*

It is time we as believers gain a greater perspective of our authority, and the full extent of the spiritual warfare raging around us. In 2 Corinthians 10:3-5, we see there are essentially three areas in which spiritual strongholds operate: (1) individual thoughts, (2) thought systems such as ideologies, philosophies, etc., and (3) geographical and political areas.

Ephesians 6:1 says, *"For we wrestle not against flesh and blood, but against principalities, against powers, against the rulers of the darkness of this world, against spiritual wickedness in high places."* In Ephesians 1:3 and verse 20, 2:6, 3:10, and 6:12, we find the Greek word "Epouranios," which is translated heavenly places. This demonstrates that spiritual battle takes place in heavenly places.

The apostle Paul talks about the **third heaven**. In 2 Corinthians 12:2, *"I knew a man in Christ above fourteen years ago, (whether in the body, I cannot tell; or whether out of the body, I cannot tell: God knoweth;) such an one caught up to the third heaven."* Paul goes on to say that he was in paradise, so we know that this was the abode of God. If there is a third heaven, logic dictates that there must also be a first and second heaven.

The Bible talks about there being **three heavens**:

The first heaven is the atmospheric heaven and clouds that surround the earth and is enjoyed by the birds that fly. This is identified in Genesis 1:8, Psalms 77:17-18, Hosea 2:18, and Psalms 19:1.

The second heaven is the abode of supernatural angelic beings, as referenced in Genesis 15:5 and Revelation 14:6. The word "midst" in the Greek is a single compound noun, and the phrase could be translated as the "the mid heaven" or "the middle heaven." This is the area of demonic attack and spiritual warfare inhabited by principalities and powers.

The third heaven, the realm of God as a place, is identified in Revelation 21:2 and 10. Revelation 4:1 is the abode of God and His angels.

In 2 Corinthians 10:4-5, Satan's mode of operation was to exercise control by the power of suggestive thought. In Acts 8:18-23, Simon was told to pray to God that the thoughts of his heart might be forgiven. The Scriptures say in Matthew 15:18-20, out of the heart proceed evil thoughts. Our thoughts are affected by everything we see or hear. Some of the corporate strongholds and thought systems that we see today are: Communism, Secular Humanism, ideals planted through print and media, and Evolution established by Charles Darwin. Satan operates in the area of suggestion; we either reject or accept the suggestion. When we accept the thought, we actually buy responsibility for the thought.

In Daniel 10:12-21, Daniel fasted for 21 days for an answer from God. However, the day he prayed, Gabriel came with the answer, but he had to battle the principalities and powers in the second heaven. He also had to call upon Michael, the archangel, the angel over Jerusalem, to come and help him in the battle. The battle took 21 earth days to win. This begins to open our eyes that the battle was in "**heavenly places**." Several other scriptures reference this concept. In Ephesians 3:10, *"To the intent that now unto the principalities and powers **in heavenly places** might be known by the church the manifold wisdom of God."* In Ephesians 6:12, we are told, *"For we wrestle not against flesh and blood, but against principalities,* *against powers, against the rulers of the darkness of this world, against spiritual wickedness **in high places**."* So these scriptures show that spiritual warfare takes place in the second heaven.

We can use our spiritual authority standing on this scripture in Matthew 16: 18-19, *"And I say unto thee, that thou art Peter, and upon this rock I will build my church; and the gates of hell shall not prevail against it. And I will give unto thee the keys of the kingdom of heaven: **and whatsoever thou shalt bind on earth shall be bound in heaven**: and whatsoever thou shalt loose on earth shall be loosed in heaven."* We have been given all authority to bind and loose any demonic activity that has hindered us. The Lord Jesus has given us power over all the power of the enemy! We need to confess, "In the name of Jesus Christ, we will not be in bondage anymore!" What we lack is not power but God's wisdom and Word spoken in the name of Jesus through our lives.

There is a time to pray and a time to declare to the powers and principalities the truth of the Word of God that has been given unto us in the name of Jesus Christ. No longer are we to pray the problem, we are to proclaim the answer. We need to be careful with the words that we speak, learning to speak only the desired end result that God's Word proclaims. God has given us His Word, which is His will for our lives. The Word of God must become alive within us by meditating it, confessing it with our mouths and believing it in our hearts. Then we will receive it as done. When we have a desire or when we pray, our faith is activated when we speak it out using the Word of God. *"We say unto that mountain be thou removed and cast into the sea."* The devil doesn't know what you are thinking since he can't read your mind. He only responds to what you are confessing or how you are expressing yourself in the flesh. Strong faith doesn't back up, it keeps going forward into the trial until it sees the victory. 2 Corinthians 4:8-13, *"We are troubled on every side, yet not distressed; we are perplexed, but not in despair; Persecuted, but not forsaken; cast down, but not destroyed; Always bearing about in the body the dying of the Lord Jesus, that the life also of Jesus might be made manifest in our body. For we which live are always delivered unto death for Jesus' sake, that the life also of Jesus might be made manifest in our mortal flesh. So then death worketh in us, but life in you. We having the same spirit of faith, according as it is written, I believed, and therefore have I spoken; we also believe, and therefore speak."*

Ephesians 1:3 states, *"Blessed be the God and Father: of our Lord Jesus Christ, who HATH BLESSED US with all spiritual blessings in heavenly places."* God has already blessed us; our confession will bring these blessings into reality when we understand about spiritual battle.

1 Peter 2:24, *"Who his own self bare our sins in his own body on the tree, that we being dead to sins, should live unto righteousness: by whose stripes ye were healed."* In understanding spiritual warfare, God's Word becomes our weapon. When we need a healing, we see that the Word states that we were healed by His stripes, so then

we confess that we are healed by the stripes of Jesus and stand on that truth. We then are no longer the sick trying to get healed, but rather the healed battling for our health, God's promised provision. We are the healed of God, not the sick of the devil. We are not to pray and ask God to heal us, but to confess that we are already healed and demand the powers and principalities of darkness to loose our healing now in Jesus name! This works for all the blessings His Word has promised.

Proverbs 6:2, *"Thou art snared with the words of thy mouth; thou art taken with the words of thy mouth."* Our negative thoughts and thinking will manifest through our negative confession. This is what is snaring most people; they continue to confess their fears, infirmities and weaknesses instead of what God has said about them. A negative confession gives the enemy the right to defeat us. The devil cannot read your mind; he can only listen to your words and watch your actions and attitude. It is through total trust in the Lord that we find freedom from the trials and tribulations of this world. Proverbs 18:21 states, *"Death and life are in the power of the tongue: and they that love it shall eat the fruit thereof."*

Satan uses natural circumstances to bring fear into your life and paralyze you. Intimidation wants to overwhelm you with a sense of inferiority and fear, which then forces you into submission and defeat. Thus, the gift of God, His spiritual ability in you, is inoperative. Now your authority has been stripped from you and will be used against you and those in the sphere of your influence.

Fear and defeat are the end result of intimidation. Satan attacks our minds through thoughts, visions, imaginations or circumstances. We also will find that if Satan cannot defeat us, he will find those closest to us to bring defeat into our lives. His whole purpose is to control and limit the ability and will of God from being manifested in our lives.

With that in mind, look at Romans 10:9-10, *"That if thou wilt confess with thy mouth the Lord Jesus, and shalt believe in thine heart that God hath raised him from the dead, thou shalt be saved"* (our profession establishes our position in the body of Christ). *"For with the heart man believeth unto righteousness; and with the mouth confession is made unto salvation."*

In Mark 11:23 God tells us, *"For verily I say unto you, That **whosoever shall say** unto this mountain, Be thou removed, and cast into the sea; **and shall not doubt in his heart, but shall believe that those things which he saith shall come to pass; he shall have whatsoever he saith**. Therefore I say unto you, **what things so ever ye desire; when you pray believe that ye receive them, and ye shall have them**."* God tells us the secret to our spiritual walk. We are to pray and confess His word into the circumstance in the name of Jesus and use our faith to believe that it will happen. It is then that we receive! We must always remember that "faith works by love," not greed, selfishness or pride.

We find this truth used by God when he created the world. In Genesis 1:1-3, *"In the beginning God, created* the heaven and earth. And the earth was without form, and void; and darkness was upon the face of the deep. And the Spirit of God moved upon the face of the waters. And **God said. Let there be light; and there was light**." The Spirit of God was the creative force that took the Word of God and created God's thoughts into substance.

Matthew 15:18-19, *"But those things which proceed out of the mouth come forth from the heart; and they defile the man. For out of the heart proceed evil thoughts, murders, adulteries, fornications, thefts, false witness, blasphemies."* If Satan can get us to speak the wrong things about our situation we will enter into agreement with him and void God's promise to us through unbelief.

Proverbs 4:20-22 says, *"My son, attend to my words; incline thine ear unto my sayings. Let them not depart from thine eyes; keep them in the midst of thine heart. For they are life unto those that find them, and health to all their flesh. Keep thy heart with all diligence; for out of it are the issues of life."* To sum this up, Jesus has done His part! He has won the victory and sent unto us the Holy Spirit. Our part is to meditate the Word of God until it comes alive within us. We have "The same Spirit of faith." 2 Corinthians 4:13, *"We having the same spirit of faith, according as it is written, I believed, and therefore have I spoken; we also believe, and therefore speak."* Victory is found when we take the Word of God and superimpose it over the thoughts of the world, the flesh and the devil. Thoughts are like seeds and will begin to grow and dominate our fears and failures. We confess the Word and believe and put our hope into what we have spoken in the name of Jesus Christ. Then we know that we will have what we say according to Mark 11:23.

CHAPTER 8

A KINGDOM OF PRIESTS

As we walk in the Kingdom of God, we are called to be a royal priesthood. God is looking for people today who will walk in the priesthood of the believer. We should be jumping for joy that God has provided the Bible for us today and has shown us through His Word this wonderful truth. But, most don't really understand what the Bible is for. Too many of us think that by reading it we are growing in the things of God. But, our growth doesn't just come by reading it. James says, *"We are to be doers of the Word and not just hearers only, deceiving ourselves."*

Revelation 1:4-6 states, *"John to the seven churches which are in Asia: Grace be unto you, and peace, from Him which is, and which was, and which is to come; and from the seven Spirits which are before the throne; and from Jesus Christ who is the faithful witness, and the first begotten of the dead, and the prince of the kings of the earth. Unto Him that loved us, and washed us from our sin in His own blood and hath made us kings and priests unto God and his Father; to*

Him be glory and dominion forever and ever." We are kings, but God is the King of kings. We can rule and reign in this life, but we are also priests, and as priests we are to bring God's love and forgiveness to this world.

What is so good about being a kingdom of priests? One of the first things is that it allows us to be led of the Spirit and not out of carnal judgment. A priest is not judgmental and insecure. A priest is not to be critical or unfair. In our need for preeminence, our pride seeks to point out the weakness or failings of others. Priests are to walk in love and leave judgment to the One Righteous Judge, who doesn't look at the outside appearance, but rather at the heart of man. Until we truly understand God's love for us, we are incapable of the righteous judgment we want for ourselves, but are not capable of giving others. In our need for pre-eminence, I'm better than you, our pride seeks to point out the weaknesses in others.

I Peter 4:8 tells us, *"Love covers a multitudes of sin."* People with a critical spirit or insecurity spend their time trying to find and expose sin, but this is not what God has called us to do. Until we grasp this revelation, we won't love one another because we will be judging one another, and whosoever sets himself as your judge denies God's right as the Righteous Judge. God looks at the heart, but we don't know where another person has been or how God is working in their lives. God tells us He doesn't judge after the outward man; God says, "I judge after the inward man." He looks on the heart.

FOUR TYPES OF LOVE

Unfortunately, in the English language, we use the word "love" for everything. We love football, we love peanut butter, we love our car, we love our wife, and we love God. However, we don't define its usage like the Greek language does, so when the Bible says to love others we truly don't have any references as to what that means. As I read the Scriptures, I began to see that the word "love" was used over and over for different translations of the Greek words for love. There are basically four different words in the Ancient Greek for love: Agape, Eros, Phileo, and Philostorgo (storge). Even though we see the word "love" translated for each of these words in many different Scriptures, the meanings of these words in the Greek differ.

Agape means a pure kind of love, which refers to a general affection or concern, rather than the physical attraction suggested by eros. Agape is a self-sacrificing, giving love to all, both friend and enemy. This is often referred to as the God kind of love, which is unconditional love. Agape appears in the New Testament to describe the relationship between Jesus and John, the beloved disciple. It also talks in Galatians 5:13 about a love for others, *"by love (agape) serve one another,"* and Ephesians 4:2 says, *"forbearing one another in love (agape),"* which is a self-sacrificing love for someone not necessarily lovely or lovable. Also, Agape is a love that acts in the best interests of someone else, such as in John 3:16, *"For God so loved (agape) the world that he gave his only begotten Son."* A Christian is required to *"love (agape) his enemies"*

Matthew 5:44. Thus, the Christian is always to do good and have the best interest of his enemies in view when he acts. Below you will see how to attain this kind of God Love.

This God kind of love "gives first" as we see in John 3:16, *"For God so loved the world, that he gave his only begotten Son, that whosoever believeth in him should not perish, but have everlasting life."* This love is not based upon our actions or performance; it is based upon God's choice to love us. So we see that agape has little to do with emotions, but has everything to do with choice. It is a love that deliberately chooses (by an act of our will) an object and loves regardless. It is an unselfish action.

1 Corinthians 13:1-8 is the "love chapter," which explains what God's kind of love truly is. These are the characteristics that the Holy Spirit wants to develop in us so that God's kind of love towards others can be manifested through our lives.

Here is the Scripture in the New King James Version. *"Though I speak with the tongues of men and of angels, but have not love, I have become sounding brass or a clanging cymbal. And though I have the gift of prophecy, and under-stand all mysteries and all knowledge, and though I have all faith, so that I could remove mountains, but have not love, I am nothing. And though I bestow all my goods to feed the poor, and though I give my body to be burned, but have not love, it profits me nothing. Love suffers long and is kind; love does not envy; love does not parade itself, is not puffed up; does not behave rudely, does not seek its own, is not provoked, thinks no evil, does not rejoice in iniquity, but rejoices in the truth;*

bears all things, believes all things, hopes all things, endures all things. Love never fails."

Verses 4-8 give us definite qualities that Jesus wants to exemplify in our lives to show the love of God. This is the mirror of the Word that causes us to examine our hearts to see if we are truly able to walk in God's love towards others. We also see that this love is an action in Romans 5:8, *"But God commendeth his love toward us, in that, while we were yet sinners, Christ died for us."* God loved us even as sinners. He initiated the relationship by reaching out to us.

Eros is a passionate love with sensual desire and longing. The Modern Greek word erotas means romantic love. This is the type of love between husbands and wives. It also is the same as sexual love. Eros is not in the Textus Receptus and although this word was most frequently used by the people living in the New Testament times, Jesus never used it and the Apostles never used it.

Phileo is a love that reacts according to how others treat you, such as what they do for you or say about you. It means friendship and is the loyalty between friends, family, and community. In the Bible, it is a brotherly love between friends such as what David and Jonathan experienced. Romans 12:10 says, *"Be kindly affectionate towards one another with brotherly love (phileo)."* A modern day usage can be seen in the name Philadelphia, "The city of brotherly love."

However, selfishness and pride are the foundation of phileo in its worldly or fallen state. We see that it is an ever-changing love since it is a selfish love based upon what I want and what I like—it's all about me and my feelings. It is about you doing what I want so that I will love (phileo) you. Phileo love is always based upon performance. Domestic violence is often the fruit of phileo love gone wrong. When phileo love goes bad, revenge enters the scene because it is an emotional love. Sadly, for some people the revenge takes the form of domestic violence or abuse—all in the name of love (phileo).

Philostorgos (storge) means affection in the Modern Greek. It is a natural affection like that felt between a mother and child or between grandparents, parents, children, etc. It is a descriptor of relationships within the family. Titus 2:4 tells us, *"admonish the young women to love (storge) their children."*

A PRIEST LOVES AND DOES NOT JUDGE

We have talked about God's identifying love in 1 Corinthians 13:1-8. This is "agape love," which is a love that is not based upon another's actions but upon one's personal decision to love. It is a love that is even higher than a parent's love for a child; it is a choice.

Practicing this type of love will allow us to grow without condemnation, and find the will of God for our lives. We will discover that God doesn't grade us on our actions and works, but on our intents and desires. When we operate as a kingdom priest, bringing people before God, we will never be offended. Now the interesting thing about the Old Testament priests is that they never looked at the people to judge them of their sins, but only to God to forgive them. The priest would receive a person's offerings, turn, bring them before God and say, "Father, forgive them. Father, bless them, sacrifice their offering and then turn around and take the next one. The role of the Priest in Leviticus 9:23-24 was to pronounce a blessing and forgiveness, which would bring joy. Today, we do not have the capability to judge one another whole-heartedly and the more we try to judge, the less we operate as a kingdom priest and the less we allow God to be the Righteous Judge. Peter denied Christ three times, and you and I would probably have said, "He wasn't really saved!" Wouldn't we? But Jesus, who came as a lifeguard to rescue people, not a Judge who condemned them, forgave him and knew that it was part of the plan of God for Peters' life. Jesus came to bring love and acceptance and forgiveness for the sinner. The purpose was to bring Peter to the end of his strength so that Jesus could be his life. Psalms 51:17 says, *"A broken and a contrite heart, O God, thou wilt not despise."* When we come to the end of our strength it is because we are broken. Too many times we want to save our life instead of lose it!

The apostle Paul said, "I'm going to appear before the righteous judge." God is the only one who knows the truth about what is going on in our hearts! It is when we are willfully violating the Word of God that the Word then judges us. If we are knowingly living in sin, the Word of God already condemns us. The Word of God has judged us. When we yield ourselves to the world we then are the world's servants. That is why we are to yield ourselves to God. If you are an average Christian like I am, then in walking out our life we will sin. I am not talking about walking in habitual sin, but we will sin, and it is then that we need someone to hold a hand out to us and help us get back on the right road. We don't need someone with a condescending attitude looking down upon us telling us we are going to hell. Our children did things against us when they were young, but we didn't condemn them to hell for it. We corrected them in love and restored our relationship. Likewise, how much more does our heavenly Father love us and want to restore our relationship? He has already held out his hand to us through Christ Jesus. Now if our children grow up and totally reject us because they are mature enough to do that, then there is nothing we can do except bless and forgive.

Romans 4:6-8, *"Now to him that worketh is the reward not reckoned of grace, but of works. But to him that worketh not, but believeth on him that justifieth the ungodly, his faith is counted for righteousness. Even as David also describeth the blessedness of the man, unto whom God imputeth righteousness without works. Saying, Blessed are they whose iniquities are forgiven, and whose sins are covered. Blessed is the man to whom the Lord will not impute sin."* This is the same attitude that a priest would have. They wouldn't judge; they would lovingly and obediently bring the sinner before God, knowing that God has already forgiven them through Christ.

John 20:21-23, *"Then said Jesus to them again, Peace be unto you: as my Father hath sent me, even so send I you. And when he had said this, he breathed on them, and saith unto them, Receive ye the Holy Ghost: Whose so ever sins ye remit, they are remitted unto them; and whose so ever sins ye retain, they are retained."* God is saying to us, if we remit or let go of someone's sins by forgiving them, they are released, but if we continue to hold on to someone's sin and operate in unforgiveness, then those sins are not forgiven. I John says, *"As he is in the world, so are we."* Jesus' purpose becomes our purpose, Jesus' power becomes our power, and Jesus' love becomes our love.

A PRIEST FORGIVES AND BLESSES

Numbers 6:22-27, *"And the Lord spoke to Moses saying: Speak to Aaron and his sons, saying, this is the way you shall bless the children of Israel. Say to them: The Lord bless you and keep you; the Lord make His face shine upon you, and be gracious to you; The Lord lift up His countenance upon you, and give you peace."* A priest was called to bless and forgive God's people. The people brought their sin offerings to the priest, and he didn't ask what their sin was and then condemn them for it. Instead, he received their offering and didn't even consider the wrongs that they had done. He sacrificed their sin offering and asked God to forgive them and bless them. The world knows that they have sinned, and they need someone to stand with them and pray, "Father, forgive them and bless them in the name of Jesus Christ." They don't need a judge; they need a priest! Some of you may have sinned today, yesterday or the day before, and you are convicted about it. You don't need me to come knocking on your door and say, "You're a sinner, and you are going to hell!" You are already convicted of your sin and don't need anyone else to try and condemn you. This is where many times we make mistakes. We try to condemn people rather than become a priest to them. They lash out at us because we too are imperfect, and we then have a yelling match. Husband and wife relationships are a good illustration of this—not mine or yours, of course, but "those other people's." We each need an understanding, loving mate who we can come to and confess our sins to without fear of judgment and condemnation. We need a priest who will stand with us in our time of confession and repentance and receive us with a loving and forgiving heart. In short, we need to become priests in our relationships, not judges! We already know that we are wrong. We are looking for someone to accept us and help us out of our situation.

In the Old Testament, a priest never judged. A priest's role was to bring that person to God. So what we learn from that is we too are to bring others—those whom God has placed in our life's path—unto God. When others sin against us, we too are to pray, "Father, forgive them and bless them in the name of Jesus." As we all begin to do this, God's Kingdom of Priests will be established, and we will become the peculiar people He was talking about. We will be peculiar because we don't try to get even; we walk in love. The priesthood of love is self-sacrificing, and love covers a multitude of sin!

Sin doesn't turn the face of God away from us because of the blood of Jesus that covers our sin, but it opens up our lives to Satan so he can come in and corrupt our lives. When we repent of our sins to the Lord, we are forgiven. True repentance means that we turn away from the sin that we were committing and make a change in our lives. John 10:10 says, *"The thief cometh not, but for to steal, and to kill, and to destroy: I am come that they might have life, and that they might have it more abundantly."* God wants to set us free from judging others and allow Him to be the one righteous judge. It seems it is easier for us to criticize others than it is to evangelize the world!

It doesn't take a lot of spiritual maturity to judge after the flesh. Simply because there is no one who is perfect, everyone can find fault with another! You now know what has separated you from those around you. Proverbs 13:10 says, *"Only by pride comes contention."* If we are walking in pride, we will be contentious. Now you know what has separated you from others—pride!

This is not the time to think you are the only one right! This is the time we need to confess our pride and learn to walk in forgiveness. Unforgiveness is a major sin in God's eyes. Why? Because we set ourselves in God's place and we become the unrighteous judge, judging after the flesh. We are called to reconcile others back to the Lord, according to Galatians 6:1, *"Brethren, if a man be overtaken in a fault, ye which are spiritual, restore such as one in the spirit of meekness; considering thyself, lest thou also be tempted. Bear ye one another's burdens, and so fulfill the law of Christ."* We are to walk in love and humility with the purpose of restoring such a one in the spirit of meekness. We are to follow Jesus' example when we pray, *"Father, forgive them for they don't know what they do."* This demonstrates the character of God and gives hope to the lost.

The Scripture in Matthew 18:15-16 also deals with being offended by someone. It says, *"Moreover if thy brother shall trespass against thee, go and tell him his fault between thee and him alone: if he shall hear thee, thou hast gained thy brother. But if he will not hear thee, then take with thee one or two more, that in the mouth of two or three witnesses every word may be established."* There are circumstances when we are unable to forgive a person, and we are instructed to talk to the person about the offense. However, we are to be diligent in judging those things in the church. Thus, when the occasion presents itself, an elder is to be rebuked before all according to 1 Timothy 5:17-20, *"Let the elders that rule well be counted worthy of double honour especially they who labour in the word and doctrine. For the scripture saith, thou shalt not muzzle the ox that treadeth out the corn. And, the laborer is worthy of his reward. Against an elder receive not an accusation, but before two or three witnesses. Them that sin rebuke before all that others also may fear."* Nowadays, it seems the church wants to cover everything up and conceal it.

In Philippians 3:12-14, the apostle Paul states, *"Not as though I had already attained, either were already perfect; but I follow after, if that I may apprehend that for which also I am apprehended of Christ Jesus. Brethren, I count not myself to have apprehended; but this one thing I do forgetting those things which are behind, and reaching forth unto those things which are before, I press toward the mark for the prize of the high calling of God in Christ Jesus."* We are in a progressive state of manifestation of God. None of us have arrived; however, we have all left the place God found us. Because of this

Jesus had to die for all of our sins, past, present and future upon the Cross. He knew that, *"there were none good, no not one."* Hopefully, we will grasp this and begin to press into the Kingdom of Priests God has called us to be rather than walking in our own judgment and condemnation of others. Generally, we do this because of our own pride, insecurities and guilt. The criterion for that is found in John 8:7, *"He that is without sin among you, let him first cast a stone at her."* We have many today who, in their pride, feel they have arrived and are walking around with a pocket full of stones. It is only when you see your own humanity that you will put down your stones and let God be the righteous judge. Let us continue to press on to know the Lord and allow Jesus to be Lord of our lives.

Let's take a minute and let me ask you this question. Who is that person, or group of persons, who have offended you? You may say to yourself, "I have every right in the world to hold a grudge against that person or persons." But, God has called us out of the world and translated us into the kingdom of His dear Son. We are called to be a Kingdom of Priests, which is the spiritual world God lives in and rules in. We are not called to hold grudges. When we can truly forgive, God also sets us free from being in bondage to our thoughts about that person or group of persons. When we can't forgive, our thoughts are brought into the captivity of the offence. You see, there is only One Righteous Judge and that is God; and you and I are not God and we certainly are not perfect. We all need people who believe in us and will stand with us during those times of temptation. Those who say, "Come on, Dan, we believe in you and know you are going to make it." They demonstrate God's love to you and choose to never leave you nor forsake you, just like God.

JOSEPH'S BETRAYAL – PART OF GOD'S PLAN

Joseph had two different dreams where he saw his family bowing down to him. His brothers became jealous of their father's love for him and planned to kill him, but instead sold him. He was taken as a slave into Egypt and was sold to Potiphar to become a servant. Joseph ended up in jail due to Potiphar's wife speaking a false accusation against him. While in jail he was able to interpret dreams. Later, when Pharaoh needed a dream interpreted, the man who had been in prison with Joseph remembered that Joseph had interpreted his dreams and told Pharaoh about him. Joseph was brought out of prison into Pharaoh's court where he interpreted the dream for Pharaoh. Joseph continued with Pharaoh and rose to be a ruler throughout all the land of Egypt. When his brethren came to Egypt to buy corn, Joseph recognized his brothers. Instead of being angry with them and resenting what they had done to him, he forgave them. He told them in Genesis 45:7-8, *"And God sent me before you to preserve you a posterity in the earth, and to save your lives by a great deliverance. So now it was not you that sent me hither, but God: and he hath made me a father to Pharaoh and lord of all his house, and a ruler throughout all the land of Egypt."* We don't know all the plans that God has for us and sometimes He uses people to get us to places that He wants us to be, which is not always a pleasant experience. But, if we have the attitude that God is behind some of the things that happen to us, we will be forgiving and press on to know Him and walk in forgiveness towards those we think have wronged us. This story helped us many times when we felt that other people could have helped us out of a challenging situation. But, if others would have done what we wanted, we would not have discovered how God could meet all of our needs. I'm sure Joseph saw how God met all of his needs no matter what he was going through, and that is why he could tell his brothers that God was the one that was behind everything that had happened to him.

A PRIEST PRAYS

Does I John 5:16 say, *"If any man see his brother sin a sin which is not unto death, he shall go up, condemn him with the Word of God, tell him that he is a dirty rotten sinner and that he is headed for hell?"* NO! It says, *"If any man see his brother sin a sin which is not unto death, he shall ask, and he shall give him life for them that sin not unto death."* So, if I see you sin, what am I to do? Pray as a priest! What example did Jesus leave us? Pray as a priest. Man's pride and insecurity says we are to expose a multitude of sins, but Proverbs tells us that love covers a multitude of sin. Isn't that what Jesus did? His love for us covered a multitude of sin in this earth so that we would no longer walk in condemnation and guilt! There are times when sin should be exposed openly, and that

155

applies to elders in the church according to I Timothy 5:19-20. Otherwise, we should walk in love toward others, lifting them up in prayer rather than openly judging, exposing and condemning them.

A world given over to darkness longs for messengers of God, members of the Royal Priesthood, who desire in the last hours of grace to save souls from the coming destruction. We do this by offering God's love, acceptance and forgiveness.

Matthew 6:9, *"After this manner therefore pray ye."* How do we pray? *"Our Father,"* which is corporately—not oh, God or My God. It says our God. It demonstrates that we are a holy nation and He is our God; there is only one God. *"Which art in heaven,"* this positionally tells us where He is. *"Hallowed be thy name,"* in the Greek language "hallowed" means to reverence the name. *"Thy kingdom come,"* for His Kingdom to come into our lives and for Jesus to reign in us and rule through us. *"Thy will be done in earth, as it is in heaven,"* God's purpose will be done in earth as it is in heaven because it's Christ reigning in us. *"Give us this day our daily bread,"* most of us want our monthly bread, look at Matthew 6:34. *"And forgive us our debts,"* (how?) *"as we forgive our debtors."* We are freed from our debts as we forgive others, acting as a Kingdom of Priests. If we don't forgive someone then we are in bondage to that person and the joy of the Lord will not be our strength, especially when we see them! You will think about them, and the negative emotion will control your life and bring bitterness into it. You will be mentally bound to any person you have not forgiven. *"Lead us not into temptation but deliver us from evil: for thine is the kingdom, and the power, and the glory, forever. Amen."*

Matthew 6:14-15, *"If you forgive men their trespasses, your heavenly Father will also forgive you: But if you forgive not men their trespasses, neither will your Father forgive your trespasses."* I want you to think about what God is saying here. He is saying, "Hey, look, there is nobody perfect; they are going to goof up, they are going to sin, they will offend you; they are going to cause you problems. But, I tell you what, you just forgive them." You should just get in a closet and say, "Father, in the name of Jesus, forgive them and bless them" because if they are not right with you, they cannot possibly be right with God. Their real problem is with their relationship with God, and you just got in the way. If our vertical relationship with God is not right, our horizontal relationship with man will not be right, either. If my relationship with God is right, my relationship with His creation—man—will also be right.

When we begin to understand this, it is then that we can become that priest for our brethren and pray forgiveness and blessings for them so that God can speak to their hearts and they can see God's love through us!

Let's look at the parable in Matthew 18:21-22, *"Then came Peter to him, and said, Lord, how oft shall my brother sin against me, and I forgive him? Till seven times? Jesus saith unto him, I say not unto thee, until seven times:*

but, until seventy times seven." Peter is beginning to understand the kingdom. He just has not allowed enough grace! As a Galilean, he was compulsive. He had a temper (which is wonderful to use against the devil, but not our fellow man), and he was really trying to be lenient. Shall I forgive him seven times? He probably thought he was being overly generous. *"But Jesus said unto him, "I say not unto thee, until seven times: but, until seventy times seven,"* (490 times). You see, Jesus was saying it is not your purpose to judge but to forgive!

In Matthew 18:23-35, Matthew speaks to us concerning binding and loosening. Jesus came to bind up the brokenhearted and to loose the captives. Forgiveness loosens the captives. Let's look at what God has done and is saying. 'Look at what I have forgiven you from. Look at the life you lived. Look at how many times you have transgressed against me, and I paid for it all, and threw it into the sea of forgetfulness, never to be remembered again.' All that sin, all that degradation of our life—He forgave it and threw it into the sea of forgetfulness, never to be remembered again. Think about that before you judge another. How are you responding to those whom God is bringing into your life to help you get free of your condescending and judgmental and critical attitude?

How are you treating Gods' family? How are you treating your family? Instead of walking in judgment, why not act like Jesus and say, "Father, forgive them and bless them." By doing this you are setting them free from your judgment and bringing them before God and allowing

Him to be their judge. Thus, you begin to understand Agape Love.

We don't always understand what another individual is going through. We need to just set them free by saying, "Father, I thank you that you have forgiven me for everything that I have done against you. This little offense that I am taking on doesn't belong to me, it belongs to Jesus; He died for the sins of the whole world. So Father, I ask that you forgive them and bless them in the name of Jesus Christ, and Father, I loose them! I loose them to your righteous judgment. I don't hold them to any debt. I just loose them, and Father I thank you that you are forgiving me as I forgive others. Thank You, Lord, I totally release them."

In Genesis 12:3, God tells us that everyone that blesses us, He will bless! Our prayer then should be, "Lord, I want to walk in your blessing and I will do so by blessing your seed, the seed of Abraham. I know that Christ is in them, so Father I ask you to forgive and bless them because, God, I want a blessed life myself. God, it is not up to me to keep track of everyone's sins. I am just going to walk in forgiveness and let you, the Righteous Judge, sort it all out. I will judge no man after my unrighteous abilities; I will command all judgment to you because you are the righteous Judge. You look at their heart. Father, you have given me the keys to the kingdom, and I loose them now from my mind and emotions and will not bind them up as debtors to me. Lord, I will not lie in bed thinking, 'How will I get even with them for what they did?' Father, I loose them and will not allow Satan to capture me with ungodly thoughts about others. God, I set the captive free and will not be bound to them, and am thankful that you will forgive me as I forgive them." We must get rid of our little scorecards; we must give them to Jesus to be truly free.

God wants us free; He is absolutely and sovereignly in control of everything, and if we will just walk in love, our lives will be blessed. God doesn't want other people controlling our emotions. He doesn't want other people having power over us. He wants us free! If you are not expecting perfection out of other people, you will never be let down. One of my quotes is, "No expectations, no disappointments!" If you will be mature enough to accept them in the position they are in, you will never go home hurt. If we leave the righteous judgment to God and believe that God is able to handle every situation, that takes faith.

Colossians 3:4, *"Christ who is our life."* God has brought Jesus back into the world to live through you. We are to walk as He walked. We are to love as He loved. We are to be His citizens in the Kingdom of God, and we are to be His Kingdom of Priests here on earth to minister His love, mercy and forgiveness to our fellow man. We see in Numbers 18:20, God gave himself completely to the priests, and they were intimately associated with Him and wholly dedicated to Him. God Himself is their inheritance. They were solely dependent upon God. From the Lord's hand material blessings come to him like manna of old as much as he needs.

CHAPTER 9

SPIRIT-FILLED BELIEVERS

Romans 14:17–19 says, *"For the kingdom of God is not meat and drink, but righteousness peace and joy in the Holy Ghost. For he that in these things serveth Christ is acceptable to God and approved of men. Let us therefore follow after the things which make for peace, and things wherewith one may edify another."* As I shared in Chapter 6, Jesus preached the kingdom of God, as did John the Baptist and Paul the apostle, so we see in the Bible that the Kingdom of God is the highest of God's callings.

Satan knows that once the church attains the revelation of the Kingdom of God and realizes that they are a holy nation, a peculiar people, a royal priesthood, a chosen generation, the body of Christ will come together fitly joined and will go about manifesting the power and ability of God on earth. So the devil knows if he can keep us fragmented and divided about the things of God, then he can disarm us. All of the denominations, groups, and churches help hinder the manifestation of the fruit of the body of Christ because we identify ourselves by our church or leader rather than the Lord. John 17:21 tells us, *"If we could be one, the world would be won."* Unfortunately, we want to major on our doctrines and set up men who we would follow instead of just allowing Jesus to be Lord of our lives. Instead, we are just as Israel who wanted to identify with Saul as opposed to the Lord. So rather than majoring on our differences, let's major and focus on the Word of God and the truth of the Kingdom.

What is the solution? We are to be doers of the Word by being willing and obedient to follow Jesus' teachings in our daily lives. We are to allow the Holy Spirit to lead us, guide us and be our helper every day.

When Jesus came into the world, He came and demonstrated the will of God through a yielded man. Jesus was the perfect manifestation of the Kingdom of God on this earth and because of that, you and I also can be born again by the Spirit of God. We can become Spirit-filled believers and go about doing the mighty works because God is now with us and in us. Remember, Jesus did not do works just for works' sake, but He only did what the Father told Him! Jesus yielded his humanity so that God's divinity could be manifested. As we learn to yield ourselves to God, we too will do the works of God (Matthew 16:24).

As we'll see in this chapter, yielding ourselves to God and being led by the Spirit require us to walk in forgiveness and obedience, and to demonstrate our new birth in Christ by growing in the Word and ministering reconciliation to the lost.

AS WE FORGIVE, GOD FORGIVES US

In Matthew 18, we find the forgiveness parable of the unmerciful servant. The servant owed the king a great debt but wasn't able to pay that debt, so the king said, *"I will forgive you this debt."* That servant then went out to collect from someone who owed him a very small debt in comparison, and threw him into jail to get his just recompense. But, verse 35 says, *"So likewise shall my heavenly Father do also unto you if you from your hearts forgive not everyone his brother their trespasses."* God reveals to us a powerful principle. If we are not responding as priests, if we are walking around holding unforgiveness for each other, that will not produce righteousness, peace and joy in our lives because we are mentally bound to somebody in a negative and unrighteous way. Satan knows that "Faith worketh by love," so he keeps us stirred up with pride, envy, strife, and division. Until you free your debtors (or anyone who has wronged you) in the name of Jesus, it is only then that you can start living as a priest; it is only then that you commit those things to God; and it is then that you sleep at night.

As the body of Christ and as royal priests we have the authority to say to those that are offending, "Father, forgive them and bless them in the name of Jesus." When Jesus was on the cross and the soldiers were gambling for His clothing, His response was, "Father, forgive them." When Stephen was being stoned, his response was, "Father, forgive them." We need to understand that when others respond to us in a negative way, their problem isn't with us, but rather with the Father. If our relationship is wrong with the Father, our relationships will be wrong with His creation. Until we are right with Him, we will not be right with one another. If we do not act as priests, we will live as legends in our own minds. II Corinthians 10:12 states that if all we do is have ourselves for company, we will appear as wise comparing ourselves among ourselves. Romans 1:22 says, *"Professing themselves to be wise they became fools."* God has put the body of Christ together to be joined together, and God has given gifts to the body so that we can all grow up in the maturity of the things of God.

Psalm 78:32, *"For all this talking they sinned still, and believed not for his wondrous works. Therefore their days did he consume in vanity, and their years in trouble. Because they would not believe God."* Where are we today in our walk with God? Have we thought about the reality of living our life through the Spirit and directed by the Word of God? The Bible is a lot like the manufacturer's handbook we get when we buy a new product. It gives us a step-by-step pattern to follow so that we operate the product in the proper manner, which will cause the product to work at its fullest capacity. So when all else fails, read the instructions. We can live our lives God's way or live our lives our way, living all our days in vanity and trouble because we are exalting our own wisdom and rejecting God's. We can live our lives by the Bible, or just make up things along the way. It is a lot like walking in a dark house without a light on. God gave us His word so that we might live a victorious life; it gives us light in this dark world.

Psalm 78:35-36 says, *"They remembered that God was their rock, and the high God their redeemer. Nevertheless they did flatter Him with their mouth, and they lied unto Him with their tongues."* This is something we can easily do today! "Oh God, if you get me out of this mess, I will never do this again. Oh God, if you let me win the lottery I will serve you all the days of my life." We all know who God is when we are in a crisis, but let everything be going our way and we soon forget. Psalm 78:37-42 says, *"Their heart was not right with Him, neither were they steadfast in His covenant. But Him being full of compassion, forgave their iniquity, and destroyed them not: yea, many a time turned He His anger away, and did not stir up all His wrath. For He remembered that they were but flesh; a wind that passeth away, and cometh not again. How oft did they provoke Him in the wilderness, and grieved Him in the desert. Yea, they turned back and tempted God, and limited the Holy One of Israel. They remembered not His hand, nor the day when He delivered them from the enemy."* One of the biggest problems we have in our relationship with the Lord is that it is dependent upon our response to His Word. The nation of Israel had come to a place that when they were in a crisis, they would call on God. But, they would not walk in His covenant and they turned away good things that were coming their way. I see many who wear the "WWJD" (what would Jesus do) bracelets, well, surely He wouldn't get himself into a lot of the messes we do!

GOD IS A REWARDER OF OBEDIENCE

We can see in Jeremiah 5:23, *"But this people hath a re-volting and rebellious heart; your iniquities have turned away these things, and your sins have withholden good things from you."* I know and am a believer that God says in John 10:10, *"The thief comes to steal, kill and destroy."* So in my life, if there is theft, if there is destruction, if there is premature death in my life, then it is the devil. But, Jesus said, very simply, *"I have come to give you an abundant life"*—a Zoë quality of life, which is not just a duration of life, but a God quality of life.

Let us look at Hebrews 11:6. God is telling us, *"We must believe that He is and that He is a rewarder of them that diligently seek Him."* We need a revelation of this. We can't go halfway. If you go halfway, and stay double-minded with your eyes on the world and also trying to see the kingdom, guess what happens? God tells us, *"A double-minded man receives nothing!"* So if nothing is going on in your life, guess what? Double-minded. We need to believe that God is and that He is a rewarder! Anything less than that will cause us to walk in foolishness and presumption and be destroyed. Jesus said, *"I come to give you an abundant life."*

As the nation of Israel stumbled through the Old Testament, limiting God, withholding reverence from God, regarding iniquity in their hearts, the Bible said the Lord would not hear them. It came to the place where their hearts were so hardened to the things of God that they couldn't believe it. The Bible says in the New Testament that God gave them over to a reprobate mind. That reprobate mind and that hardened heart say, "You can go do all the things of the world and it is okay," and they'll believe that. I have had people in counseling who believe they can live like the devil and still be blessed of the Lord. But, it doesn't work. The reason they believe that is they have a reprobate mind; they believe the life they live is fine, regardless of what God said, and they come to a place in their life where they run into a major crisis and are destroyed because they lack the knowledge that sets them free. It is just like the Law of Gravity; we can't change it. If we jump off of a building, we will fall and hurt ourselves. It's a law that has no respect of persons. So it is with the Kingdom and the laws of God. Acts 10:34, *"Then Peter opened his mouth, and said, Of a truth I perceive that God is no respecter of persons."*

NEW CREATURE IN CHRIST

We have found that the Kingdom of God, according to Romans 14:17, is righteousness, peace and joy in the Holy Ghost. Now to come into that place, we want to understand that we have become a new creation in Christ—old things have passed away and we have been reconciled unto God as we are told in 2 Corinthians 5:17. **We are now a new creation; (in the Greek it says "one who has never existed before") humanity and deity have been joined together.** We are to die to our humanity so that God can now live and manifest himself through our mortal bodies.

Matthew 10:7-8 says, *"Going into all the world, casting out devils, laying hands on the sick"*—now, that's the program for evangelism. This will work in your neighborhood. This will work with your friends. If we demonstrate the power of God, and what should be a transformed life, the world wouldn't be walking in darkness.

Let Jesus live His life through you by believing the Word and cast down those imaginations and strongholds that say, "I want to live my life," and start trusting God! We are to be a part of the Kingdom of Priests because the Kingdom of God is at hand—it is not in word, it is not in man's wisdom—it's in the power and demonstration of the Holy Spirit. That's when you will see people getting delivered because the Kingdom of God is now and is in you.

You might as well pull your head out of the sand and be about your Father's business and have holy boldness because God is a rewarder. God wants to reward you with more people for you to minister to. He wants to develop a ministry in you, within and without, so you could go about serving people and be prosperous in the Kingdom of God. That's what God wants out of our lives. He wants us to minister in all the earth. He wants us to grasp hold of the basic tools of evangelism. According to the Bible, evangelism isn't knocking on doors, asking people if they are saved. It is going forth in the power and the might of God. Let's look at 2 Corinthians 5:14, *"For the love of Christ constraineth us,"* (this means it urged us, it presses us on) *"because we thus judge, that if one died for all, then were all dead."* Jesus was a substitute. He died for the sins of the whole world. He has already died for the sins of the whole world, but the world has to receive him. *"And that he died for all, that they which live should not henceforth live unto themselves, but unto him which died for them, and rose again."*

RESULTS OF BEING BORN AGAIN

What are some of the results of being born again? We begin to no longer live unto ourselves, but unto Him. It is very simple; if you are an apple tree you produce apples, not oranges, not grapefruit, not figs. You produce the fruit of your life, your roots. It is black and white; or should we say darkness and light. We are delivered out of the power of darkness and brought into His marvelous light. If I am walking in darkness, then my life will manifest it; I am a servant of darkness. Jesus comes into us, and He is the author and finisher of our faith. It is Him that worketh within us. I know whose I am because of the life that I live, and it is no longer my life that I live, but it is Christ living in me. Galatians 5:13-16 says, *"For brethren, ye have been called unto liberty; only use not liberty for an occasion to the flesh, but by love serve one another. For all the law is fulfilled in one word, even in this; Thou shalt love thy neighbour as thyself. But if ye bite and devour one another, take heed that ye be not consumed one of another. This I say then, walk in the spirit, and ye shall not fulfill the lust of the flesh."*

They didn't know if you would look into the gospels you could see the church of Jesus Christ. At that time, Jesus only demonstrated to them in the flesh through signs, wonders and miracles, through seeing, and through hearing the things that were testified about. They only saw Jesus in the flesh, but a spiritual revelation came to them saying, Jesus is the Son of God.

Let's go back to 2 Corinthians 5:17-18, *"Therefore, if any man be in Christ, he is a new creature; old things are passed away; behold, all things are become new. And all things are of God, who hath (past tense) reconciled us to himself by Jesus Christ, and hath given to us the ministry of reconciliation."* Jesus said in John 8:12, *"I am the light of life."* Isn't that good news? Because Jesus is the light of the world, you and I, who are born of the Spirit of God, don't walk in darkness. That's great news! You see, the Kingdom of God is in us. There is not a local church, there is not a major denomination, there is not one country, but the Kingdom of God encompasses the whole world. People impacted by God who walk in love living their lives through the mind of Christ.

Why is it that we think in America, where 94% of the ministers minister to 6% of the people in the world, they still need to feed us? I believe it is time for the church to quit worrying about being fed and get out and be led by the Spirit of God to go and do the works of Jesus. I believe the time is now. I don't believe it is time to sit around and vegetate in a church someplace trying to get deeper and deeper into God. I say, go out and allow God to use your life for His purposes. Besides, true maturity is being a doer of the Word and walking in love. Praise God! God is looking for laborers! He said, "Pray ye the Lord of the harvest and I'll send laborers," and I believe God is sending laborers into the field.

When I allowed Jesus to be Lord, I went. I began to seek out what He wanted me to do. First I studied the Bible, reading it through in three months, and then dissecting it so that I could understand what God was telling us in His handbook.

I was still working a job, but when He told me to go preach, I preached. My ministry started by sharing at faith meetings and preaching at various churches. Then God moved me to Colorado where I began to teach in a campground on Sunday Mornings. When He says, "Go," we need to go!

The average person in the average denominational church may come to church 50 Sundays a year. In the average church, the message is about 30 minutes—that means the average person attending church over a period of a year gets about 25 hours of teaching in a year. But, the big problem with that is most people in an average church zone out 15 minutes of every message...don't they? That means then, the average Sunday Christian who's coming to church and getting the half hour program is now getting 12-½ hours of teaching a year, but you and I know that we don't retain 100% of what we hear...do we? By the time we get to the door, get into our car, and go down the hill, we have forgotten half of the 15 minutes we already heard. So the average person in a year hears the gospel about six hours. Do you know they spend more time in one day watching television than getting Bible teaching in an entire year if they don't study for themselves at home? We look at this nation and say, "Why is this a carnal nation?" Because the average Christian gets six hours of teaching a year and then destroys that with negativity from the radio and television and newspapers and communication. So the average Christian, if he is not applying himself in the doing of this thing, actually goes and becomes more carnal as the years go by. Faith without action is dead; we need to be doers of the Word, not hearers only.

GROWTH RESULTS

There is something I have noticed since being in the pastoral ministry since 1976 regarding the correlation of time spent in the Word and the kind of seed that is planted in a person. Of course, there are exceptions to every opinion. I must admit this may be a subject of debate. It seems three years is about the period of time in which you look at a new believer's life to ascertain what kind of seed is planted in them.

First Year   The new believer is excited, and there is joy. There is a desire to know God and to please Him.

Second   If the believer is regularly getting into the Word, he or she is gaining knowledge and wisdom and growing in the Lord.

Third Year   If the believer has continued in the Word, he or she has been set free from wrong thinking and begins following Jesus' example by manifesting the power and ability of God, and touching the lives of those around them and seeing them changed.

Science today says that the brain cells in our bodies change every three years. This could explain that by renewing our minds it totally changes who we are. In that three-year period, those who stay in the Word will be doers of the Word and go on to become great men and women of God. But, those who do not stay in the Word during that three-year period end up back into darkness, wandering around, saying, 'it didn't work for me.' This is one reason it is so important to disciple new believers, to come alongside them and encourage them in the Word, and to testify how God has worked in your life. Once a new believer begins to build a history with God and see His Word and promises spring to life, there is no turning back!

Jesus is no respecter of persons; He isn't going to give me greater revelation in the Word of God than He is going to give you. We all start at the same level; it's what you are doing with the time that you have. The Kingdom of God is crying out for laborers, people who will go out into the earth and say, "brother, sister, I want to tell you about Jesus. He'll forgive your sins and change your life. You can be reconciled back unto God." This means that peace is made with God by the sacrifice of Jesus Christ. When I first ministered in Guatemala, I gave the altar call and when I opened my eyes, I was surrounded by so many people wanting a touch from Jesus Christ that I couldn't move. People were being healed. Some people would say, "I don't believe in healing." Well, praise God, I've seen too much to doubt it now. There was a time when I wondered, but I know it is real. The power of God is available today for you and me..

MINISTRY OF RECONCILIATION

We all have been given a ministry. What's that ministry? We are His ambassadors, and our purpose is to reconcile the world back to God through Jesus Christ. 2 Corinthians 5:20-21, *"We are ambassadors for Christ, as though God did beseech you by us: we pray you in Christ's stead, be ye reconciled to God. For He hath made Him to be sin for us, who knew no sin; that we might be made the righteousness of God in Him."* Romans 14:17 says, *"The Kingdom of God is not meat nor drink, but it is righteousness."* As we look at this, righteousness is translated as right standing.

Jesus was made sin. This, then, is our identification that we might be made the righteousness of God in Him— or the right standing or right doing of God in Him. How, then, do I receive the righteousness to see the Kingdom of God? Where's that righteousness? It's in Jesus. Isn't it? You see, there is identification. Jesus identified with fallen man in that He identified with their sin, and He carried all of that sin to the cross and He died. He carried all of our sins into hell, paid the penalty for that and then ascended back to heaven. Our response to Jesus' action is that we receive Him. We say, "Lord Jesus, I recognize myself as a sinner. I know that I am not righteous before God, but I accept your completed works, the right doing that you did for my life, and I ask forgiveness and I commit my life and make you Lord of my life." What then, did we receive besides salvation? Righteousness.

Let's go back and look at Romans 3:21, *"But now the righteousness of God without the law is manifested, being witnessed by the law and the prophets; Even the righteousness of God which is by faith..."* That means faith is trusting in and adhering to the Word of God, and I expect it to be true and to have tangible results. By receiving Jesus Christ I receive the righteousness, this verse continues, *"of Jesus Christ unto all and upon all them that believe."* It is a verb; it demands action, so you have to respond. You can't come down here and pray, "Oh, Lord Jesus, come into my life, save me from hell in Jesus name, amen," and go out the door and live like the devil. You are not saved. Salvation demands action. Salvation is dependant upon our repentance; it is a new life living in you! Until there is repentance, there is no salvation. Repent, turn from your sins, for all have sinned and come short of the glory of God. That means every one of us.

All of us are lumped into that category. Romans 3:24-26, *"Being justified freely by his grace through the redemption that is in Christ Jesus: whom God hath set forth to be a propitiation through faith in his blood, to declare his righteousness for the remission of sins that are past through the forbearance of God; to declare, I say at this time his righteousness that he might be just and the justifier of him which believeth in Jesus."*

The Old Testament Church, the nation of Israel, was never righteous because they went about trying to establish their own righteousness. Hebrews 10:3 brings that out. They wouldn't walk in what God had intended for them, and rejected Him. So God, according to Matthew in the New Testament, has taken away the Kingdom of God from the nation of Israel, and has given it to another nation that will bear forth the fruit of the Spirit of God through their lives. Hosea 6:4 says, *"My people are destroyed for their lack of knowledge,"* because they rejected him. People today are destroyed, not because the knowledge isn't there. It's because they reject the Word of God and want to stand in their own wisdom. That's pretty scary when we exalt ourselves above God. It doesn't work. Let's look at Romans 5. We find where righteousness again counts. Verse 15, *"But not as the offense, so also in the free gift. For if through the offense of one (Adam) many be dead, much more the grace of God, and the gift by grace, which is by one man, Jesus Christ, hath abounded unto many. And not as it was by one that sinned, so is the gift: for the judgment was by one to condemnation, but the free gift is of many offenses unto justification. For if by one man's offense death reigned by one: much more they which receive abundance of grace and the gift of righteousness, the gift of right standing."* They shall reign. Does that sound like you are to be downtrodden and defeated? Does that sound like a glorious gospel?

We are to reign in life by one, Christ Jesus. That means we are to understand Jesus has already won our victory so that we might reign in life over our circumstances and over the power of the devil. That means we may have a rewarding life and be prosperous in serving people as we live as priests. The greatest blessing we can have is ministering life and health to people and serving them by the will of God. This truly begins in our own families. The world says to forget your family and go out and be something great, get your head in a cloud and let your family go to hell. But, God tells you to reconcile your family, to minister life to your family. We reconcile that family unit first. It's the home that's always the first place of ministry. It is always the home. That is the mirror of our spiritual condition. But, the world tries to tear the family unit apart by attacking our children. Then we think, those kids, you can't do anything with them, they are just that way. The demonstration of the Gospel is seen in what is happening in your own family. For elders in the church, that becomes our first responsibility according to the gospel of the Lord Jesus Christ (Titus 1:6). That's the first place of ministry. That's the good news.

Jesus came to give us righteousness so we might have right standing with God. This means when I pray I might come boldly before the throne of grace and know that God is going to hear my prayers because I have right relationship with Him through the cross of Jesus. I then know that I can be as bold as a lion because I am righteous because of what Jesus has done. Once you understand and recognize it is a free gift, you can receive it.

As Paul says, "Do we continue in sin? God forbid." In my own life, the day I was born again was the greatest day in my life because I became clean. I had the opportunity to live life again, to start all over and lay down my past and become a new creation. Once you put on that white garment of the Lord Jesus Christ, the last thing you want is a bunch of spots and wrinkles in it. Once you can see yourself cleansed by what Jesus has done, you don't ever want to get dirty again. I looked at my old garment;

it was so dirty, wrinkled and polluted that it was pure joy to take it off and receive the Lord Jesus' white garment. Jesus said, "I don't care what you did yesterday, I don't care what your life was like, you are now clean." Jesus reconciled us back to the Father.

Jesus' righteousness became my righteousness and once I became clean, I wanted to stay that way. That's why we are born again. We are given another chance at life. We are given the chance to accept the power and ability of God and His righteousness, and the Kingdom of God is first of all righteousness. We are given the chance of living our lives through the power of His life within us! What an awesome God we serve, who loved us and gave himself for us.

Now we see that being a Spirit-filled believer is a lifestyle. It is yielding our will to God, following the Bible and allowing Jesus to work through us. Our Spirit-filled position heightens our awareness of the Kingdom of God and allows us to walk fully in the provision, prosperity and power of the Lord as His ambassadors and priests here on earth.

CHAPTER 10

BLESSINGS OF LIVING IN THE KINGDOM OF GOD

Throughout the Scriptures we see that God wants to bless his children by giving them an abundant life: clothing, shelter, food, and also peace, joy, healing, deliverance from the enemy and every wonderful thing that heaven holds. Penny experienced this in a most wonderful way when she was first born again. We had no money to buy anything extra, but Penny asked the Lord to give her longer dresses for church as she only had miniskirts, which the Lord revealed to her were no longer appropriate. A lady invited her over to her house and had what looked like her whole wardrobe laid out on the bed. She told Penny to take what she wanted because it was all going to Goodwill. Penny came home with all of her clothes. What a mighty God we serve! We were beginning to see the blessings of living in the Kingdom of God. Throughout our walk there were other blessings that had to do with needs of clothing. Our oldest daughter was outgrowing her clothing, Penny prayed and God provided through someone who didn't even know that we had a need. When God provides,

He doesn't leave anything out. He made sure we had shoes, socks, coats, etc. We had given up everything to follow Him.

God also provided different places for us to live. We may have thought that we were providing our own shelters, but as we look back we can see God's hand as He led people into our lives that provided temporary shelter while we were making transitions. When we first moved to Colorado Springs and were looking for a home to rent, the first place we considered looking at was a 5-bedroom home. As we talked, we decided that was too big for us, so we didn't look at it. But, after looking at homes all day, we went back to that home. While sitting in front of it waiting for the landlord, Penny opened her Bible to a Scripture that said, *"I have prepared a place for you!"* We knew we were at the right place then. That is how simply God can lead us if we allow Him to speak to us. We may have thought the house was too big, but God used it for Bible studies and ministering to a lot of people. Our extra bedrooms were filled by many who stayed with us.

As I reminisce on the blessings that Penny and I received as a result of turning over our lives to Him, I'm reminded of the many times we were in situations that we couldn't go forward at all unless God intervened with an answer. We prayed about every circumstance that arose in our lives and watched as God brought answers to each prayer. Maybe not in the way we expected, but He truly brought us through every problem we faced.

Food was another area that God said He would take care of. At one point we were completely out of food and had no money. A knock on the door brought a lady who had many bags of groceries and thought she may not have heard from God correctly because people assumed we were doing well. This was due to the fact that we never told people our problems—we only took them straight to God! Another gentlemen would drop by often and bring us day old bread and other bread products. Thank God for His servants who truly hear His voice. So God really took care of all of our needs: food, clothing, and shelter. As God met every need, it caused us to have the faith to pray for others and faithfully do the work of the ministry. We knew that God would meet their needs just as He was meeting ours.

Peace and joy are also blessings from the Lord as we live in His Kingdom. Many will experience different emotions as they enter into Kingdom living, but peace is supernatural. Our natural man does not know how to have peace at all times and keep it through every kind of situation. Penny was a worrier, but she began to experience this peace and couldn't worry at all for a period of time. She was so refreshed joy became a fruit in her life. This is what God wants for us: to be able to cast all of our cares upon him and not consider all of the fears that may keep trying to hound us. The opposite of peace is turmoil, which many people live in most of their lives. But, God came to set us free from any emotion that steals peace from us.

We see that God wants to give us this abundant life, but most of all God wants to reveal himself to us in a personal way, which is true prosperity. When God's life is manifested through our mortal bodies, His will can be done on earth as it is in heaven. As we learn from the Scriptures of Jesus' life, we begin to see Jesus is to become our life. We will discover that our destiny is in the hands of God, and that He is perfecting His purpose and His will through our life. Our life in the flesh no longer matters, and the will of God becomes our passion. (For example, you begin to realize if God wanted me to have more, I would have had more. Maybe, God had given me all I needed and, because of the power of choice, I decided to act on my own will and mismanaged the finances God had given me.) Our purpose is not to press in to get more from God, but rather to be conformed into the image of His Son and learn to walk in love and contentment. The Sermon on the Mount was preached so that people could see the blessings of living in the Kingdom of God, which are also referred to as the Beatitudes.

THE BEATITUDES

Christ came once in the flesh and He is coming yet again soon. His second coming will be for the purpose of setting up His Kingdom in glory. It is therefore vitally important that we understand what the character of the subjects in the Kingdom are, so that we may know whether we belong to the Kingdom ourselves and whether its privileges, immunities and future rewards are a part of our present and future inheritance. The Beatitudes describe the character and conduct of a Christian; Jesus is the perfect pattern. Jesus unveils and announces the problem and the solution for mankind. He is the perfect pattern.

As we in the United States of America have our government's constitution, the Bible has its constitution for the Kingdom of God. Found in Matthew 5:2-12, the Beatitudes list attributes God says can be in our lives if we press in to know Jesus. The book of Matthew was written to the Jews, who didn't like to talk about God because they thought it was blasphemous. In this book is the only place we see the Kingdom of heaven dealt with directly and continually, while the rest of the Word refers to the Kingdom of God. Let's review the Beatitudes, keeping in mind that this teaching is from Jesus Himself.

> *"And he taught them saying, "Blessed are the poor in spirit,"* those who recognize their own spiritual insufficiency and helplessness, *"for theirs is the kingdom of heaven."* To those of us who are poor in spirit and recognize that we are spiritually helpless, to us is the Kingdom of heaven.

> *"Blessed are they that mourn; for they shall be comforted."* Here, those that mourn are those dealing with unhappiness due to sorrow over their own sins or the sins of others, as well as the awfulness of our sins against God, The good news is God says He will comfort them. He is just waiting for us to turn to Him and cry out so He can be there for us in our times of mourning.

> *"Blessed are the meek for they shall inherit the earth."* This was an interesting thought for me

because I spent my earlier life being dominant, taking what I wanted and living my life my way. Then I saw that God wanted me to be meek (not to be confused with weakness), we are to be bold and strong and very courageous in the Lord. Meek, meaning what? Weak in my own fleshly strength so He can give me His strength. When I "help" Him out, He withholds because He doesn't want my flesh to be mixed into the pot. It's all God. The Lord is looking for humility and submission to Him, and not so concerned about our will and our way.

"Blessed are they which do hunger and thirst after righteousness: for they shall be filled." When we search the Scriptures for truth and answers because there is a hunger and a thirst inside of us, He promises that we will be filled. The foundation requirement for all Godly living is to "hunger and thirst after righteousness." When the eye of the soul is turned away from self to God and we begin to long after righteousness. This will cause us to be sensitive to the Holy Spirit's leading in our lives.

"Blessed are the merciful: for they shall obtain mercy." This becomes the character of genuine disciples. A person already hates themselves for what they have done. They don't need our help in judgement. Mercy flows from the heart that is captured by and in love with the mercy of God.

The same mercy that the Lord has given you is the mercy we are to give to others who have failed. Galatians 6:1, *"Brethren, if a man be overtaken in a fault, ye which are spiritual, restore such a one in the spirit of meekness; considering thyself, lest thou be tempted."* Jesus came to establish love, mercy and forgiveness to those seeking Him. The only ones He condemned were the religious Pharisees. Always pray to have eyes that see the best in people—a heart that forgives the worst, a mind that forgets the bad, and a soul that never loses faith in God. As we show mercy to others, God will be merciful to us.

"Blessed are the pure in heart: for they shall see God." What is purity? It is the freedom from defilement and divided affections; it is sincerity and genuineness with singleness of heart. To obtain a pure heart is a continuous process as we keep the Word and get free of the things that keep us in bondage. We are seeking to have the same attitude as God has, a love for righteousness and a hatred for evil. Thus, the purer our heart is, the more clearly we can see God at work in our lives. The more our hearts are made pure the more we will see the Lord in our daily lives.

"Blessed are the peacemakers for they shall be called the children of God." Jesus calls us peacemakers because within us is a desire to see all come to know God and bring the peace of God

to them we ourselves have experienced. We recognize that we have been reconciled by the Lord and live our lives to bring others into this relationship with Him. This attribute gives completeness or wholeness to Christian character. The Lord has sent us as ambassadors of peace into the world. Knowing God as our father and we as His family, we live our lives to bring others into this relationship with the Father.

"Blessed are they which are persecuted for righteousness' sake for theirs is the kingdom of heaven." As believers we will soon realize that persecution is from Satan and is intended to uproot God's Word from our lives, Mark 4:16-17. This is not talking about being persecuted for just any reason. No, it refers to being persecuted for being a believer in Christ Jesus. Persecution is from Satan and is intended to uproot God's Word in our lives. When we are persecuted for our faith, then we are blessed.

"Blessed are ye when men shall revile (verbally abuse) you and persecute you and shall say all manner of evil against you falsely, for my sake." We are blessed when we are being reviled or persecuted because of following Jesus, not for any other reason. We find in Acts 9:4 that it is not you that they are persecuting, but Christ in you. In II Timothy 3:12 it tells us that "All that will live godly in Christ Jesus shall suffer persecution."

The only ones who don't suffer persecution are those that live worldly.

"Rejoice, and be exceeding glad: for great is your reward in heaven: for so persecuted they the prophets which were before you." It's not always easy to rejoice when people are coming against you, but there is a reward awaiting us for our perseverance. These nine beatitudes teach us the attributes that Jesus wants to see in our lives.

Jesus began his ministry teaching the beatitudes and as you meditate on them you will begin to see for yourself the nature that God has for us. It's not about us doing our own religious works. In Matthew 16:24 it is about us abandoning all that we are, denying ourselves and taking up our cross and following Jesus. As we work toward this goal, keep these things in mind:

- We need to earnestly contend for the relationship that began 2000 years ago.

- Don't let the enemy bring you into a new and temporary religion.

- Go back to your Bibles, go back to Jesus and allow him to be Lord.

- Allow His purpose to be lived through you.

- Put your confidence in Him.

- Become convinced, rock-solid convinced that the unseen things of God are real.

- Don't move until He tells you to move.

- Be still until you know that He is going to be God in that issue and allow your faith to rise.

- Become that man or woman of God so when you stand before Him He will say, "Well done, thou good and faith-filled servant."

These Beatitudes teach us the attributes that Jesus wants to see in our lives. Jesus began His ministry teaching the beatitudes and as we meditate on them we begin to see for ourselves the true nature of God.

You see, it's real! Now I want to give you a secret, our God reigns. All that He says is true. Everything He does for others, He will do for you. This is an awesome God we serve.

KINGDOM OF SERVANTS

Being great in God's Kingdom is not the same as being great in the eyes of man. Much today in the church world has been done to promote men into a position of leadership and power, yet in God's Kingdom He would not call that greatness. His concept of greatness has been totally overlooked, and just as the nation of Israel did not want an invisible God to lead them, we find the same thing in our churches today.

The people are looking for heroes, such as Israel's King Saul who stood head and shoulders above the rest of them and demonstrated courage, power and strength in their eyes. But, as in the days of Israel, that is not what God desires for us.

Today God is not interested in these physical attributes, but is looking for servant leadership. Mark 10:44 says, *"And whosoever of you will be the chiefest, shall be servant of all. For even the Son of man came not to be ministered unto, but to minister, and to give his life a ransom for many."* He states that greatness is found in the heart of His servants. If we truly want to be great we must become the servant of them all. John 13:34-35 tells us, *"A new commandment I give unto you, That ye love one another; as I have loved you, that ye also love one another. By this shall all men know that ye are my disciples, if ye have love one to another."* Jesus also spoke this in John 17:21, *"That they all may be one; as thou, Father, art in me, and I in thee, that they also may be one in us: that the world may believe that thou hast sent me. It is in walking in love that the truth of God will be established in this world."* He also states in I John 3:16, *"Hereby perceive we the love of God, because he laid down his life for us: and we ought to lay down our lives for the brethren."*

Jesus has called us to follow His example and a couple of Scriptures bring this out very clearly. Luke 9:23-26 says, *"And he said to them all, If any man will come after me, let him deny himself, and take up his cross daily, and follow me. For whosoever will save his life shall lose it: but whosoever will lose his life for my sake, the same shall save it. For what is a man advantaged, if he gain the whole world, and lose himself, or be cast away? For whosoever shall be ashamed of me and of my words, of him shall the Son of man be ashamed, when he shall come in his own glory, and in his Father's, and of the holy angels."* He also brings it out in Matthew 25:31-46, *"When the Son of man shall come in his glory, and all the holy angels with him, then shall he sit upon the throne of his glory: And before him shall be gathered all nations: and he shall separate them one from another, as a shepherd divideth his sheep from the goats: And he shall set the sheep on his right hand, but the goats on the left. Then shall the King say unto them on his right hand, Come, ye blessed of my Father, inherit the kingdom prepared for you from the foundation of the world: For I was an hungered, and ye gave me meat: I was thirsty, and ye gave me drink: I was a stranger, and ye took me in: Naked, and ye clothed me: I was sick, and ye visited me: I was in prison, and ye came unto me. Then shall the righteous answer him, saying, Lord, when saw we thee an hungered, and fed thee? or thirsty, and gave thee drink? When saw we thee a stranger, and took thee in? or naked, and clothed thee? Or when saw we thee sick, or in prison, and came unto thee? And the King shall answer and say unto them, Verily I say unto you, Inasmuch as ye have done it unto one of the least of these my brethren, ye have done it unto me. Then shall he say also unto them on the left hand, Depart from me, ye cursed, into everlasting fire, prepared for the devil and his angels: For I was an hungered, and ye gave me no meat: I was thirsty, and ye gave me no drink: I was a stranger, and ye took me not in: naked, and ye clothed me not: sick, and in prison, and ye visited me not. Then shall they also answer him, saying, Lord, when saw we thee an hungered, or athirst, or a stranger, or naked, or sick, or in prison, and did not minister unto thee? Then shall he answer them, saying, Verily I say unto you, Inasmuch as ye did it not to one of the least of these, ye did it not to me. And these shall go away into everlasting punishment: but the righteous into life eternal."* It amazes me what we think Christianity is today because when we look at the Word of God we find just the opposite. We see people who have laid down their lives and are giving up everything for the purpose of God in their lives. It seems we would rather just go to our local church and criticize our fellow believers than to serve the needs of others.

Let's let Jesus sum it up in His own words. He says in Matthew 23:10-12, *"Neither be ye called masters: for one is your Master, even Christ. But he that is greatest among you shall be your servant. And whosoever shall exalt himself shall be abased; and he that shall humble himself shall be exalted."*

From the foundations of the earth, God had a purpose for us. We find that purpose in the Old Testament in Exodus 19:3-6, *"And Moses went up unto God, and the Lord, called unto him out of the mountain, saying, Thus shalt thou say to the house of Jacob, and tell the children of Israel; Ye have seen what I did unto the Egyptians, and how I bare you on eagles wings, and brought you into myself. Now therefore, if ye will obey my voice indeed, and keep my covenant, then ye shall be a peculiar treasure unto me above all people: for all the earth is mine: And ye shall be unto me a kingdom of priests, and an holy nation. These are the words which thou shalt speak unto the children of Israel."* God wants His life to be manifested through our mortal bodies. He wants His ways to find entrance into the earth through His people. We are the vehicles God wants to use for His will to be done on earth as it is in heaven.

ANOINTED TO HEAL, DELIVER, CAST OUT DEVILS, SPEAK WITH NEW TONGUES

In 1 John 20:21, Jesus told his disciples, *"As the Father sent me, so send I you."* In Romans 12:1 we are instructed, *"to present our bodies a living sacrifice to God."* What does this mean? We are to present our bodies unto God, to be empowered by His Holy Spirit, so that we may be about His business. That is the living sacrifice; we sacrifice our ways, wills and purposes and let God use our lives for His will. Putting down our nature, putting down our desires, putting down our earthly treasures and pursuits and being about the Father's business. It is in this lifetime that we lay up treasures in heaven. Today, we need to hear what the Spirit is saying to the church.

Penny and I both really wanted to present our bodies as a living sacrifice to God and to be empowered by His Holy Spirit. We began the process of changing our ways to be more like Jesus, and we also decided to trust Jesus totally with our lives. As we studied the Word, we began to understand that God wanted to provide for us. At that time, I had just gotten out of the motel-restaurant business and was managing a gas station. We knew that such a huge step of faith would really cause the blessings of God to pour out on us, but we also knew the struggle of survival would be a real test. Yet, because we were following God, we had the blessing of joy unspeakable during that time.

Another blessing that God showed us was to trust Him for healing rather than running to the doctors for everything.

It was easy to run to the doctors when we had insurance, but at this time we no longer were able to carry insurance and, understandably, Penny had a lot of fear every time the girls had a fever or coughed. So our faith and trust in God had to grow. We began to pray for healing over our family, and prayer was working. We began to see them healed quickly. God healed Penny's back, a cyst on her body, her tooth and provided many other miracles in our family. We felt so happy to be a family serving God and knew that we had a calling on our lives.

Faith was another great blessing as God gave both Penny and I the gift of faith to believe God would take care of us no matter what came our way. It is interesting that God begins doing seemingly little things that produce great faith in our lives. As Oral Roberts taught us, "Expect a Miracle." Now we had faith to believe that God wanted us healed, that He would provide the funds when we had a financial need, that He would provide the right homes for us to live in, and that He would provide food and other necessities of our lives.

Acts 10:38 tells us, *"For God hath anointed Jesus of Nazareth,"* (God anointed Jesus the man; when the Word speaks of Jesus of Nazareth it is talking about the humanity of our Savior) *"with the Holy Ghost and power; who went about doing good, and healing all that were oppressed of the devil; for God was with Him."* As I look at that Scripture it says to me, "for God hath anointed Dan of Colorado Springs!" He has anointed each of us, wherever we live, with the Holy Ghost and power that we might do good, healing all that are oppressed by the devil because God is with us.

Deliverance is another blessing from the Lord as He desires to set people free from Satan's grip of entanglement in alcohol, drugs, depression, etc. God wants to use His people to bring the good news that Jesus came to set them free. People carry hurts from past experiences or events in their lives, and Jesus wants to bring healing to the brokenhearted and those bruised and wounded in their emotions.

Luke 4:16 says, *"And he came to Nazareth, where he had been brought up: and, as his custom was, he went into the synagogue on the Sabbath day, and stood up for to read. And there was delivered unto him the book of the prophet Esaias. And when he had opened the book, he found the place where it was written, The Spirit of the Lord is upon me, because he hath anointed me to preach the gospel to the poor; he hath sent me to heal the brokenhearted, to preach deliverance to the captives, and recovering of sight to the blind, to set at liberty them that are bruised, To preach the acceptable year of the Lord. And he closed the book, and he gave it again to the minister, and sat down. And the eyes of all them that were in the synagogue were fastened on him. And he began to say unto them, this day is this Scripture fulfilled in your ears."*

God has a calling on our lives to preach the gospel to the poor, to heal the brokenhearted, to preach deliverance to the captives and sight to the blind and liberty to them that are bruised. When we allow ourselves to be His vessels, we will begin to act more like Jesus.

God said He would take the Kingdom away from the Jews and give it to a nation bringing forth fruit. Matthew

21:43 states this, *"Say I unto you, The Kingdom of God shall be taken from you, and given to a nation bringing forth the fruits thereof."* Matthew 28:18-19 focuses on the commandment for the Kingdom of God, *"And Jesus came and spake unto them, saying, "All power is given unto me in heaven and in earth. Go ye therefore, and teach all nations, baptizing them in the name of the Father, and of the Son, and of the Holy Ghost: Teaching them to observe all things whatsoever I have commanded you."* What did He command them to do? He told them to cast out devils, lay hands on the sick, preach deliverance and speak in new tongues. He told them this is the Kingdom of God on this earth. He told there is a God that so loved them He wanted to produce in their life supernatural power. There is a God that so loved them He wanted to financially take care of them. There is a God who so loved us He wanted us to have His ability to love. There is a God who so loves you that He wants to give you love, acceptance and forgiveness for all the sins of your life and let you begin again.

I have had the joy of traveling to many nations and have discovered that God's Kingdom is in all places and people. There are people who have submitted their lives to the lordship of Jesus Christ, God's Kingdom has been established in their lives, and they are going about the Father's business. We become the hands and legs and mouth that God uses in this world to establish His kingdom in the hearts of his people. It is when we allow the lordship of Jesus in our lives that we enter into the blessings of the Kingdom.

Proverbs 4:20 talks about how the *"Word of God is life and health to those that find it."* Do you know why those that

195

find it have life and health? Because they are His disciples indeed and they did continue in the Word of God. God brought His Word to this earth, and we live in an age where if you apply it to your life, you will be victorious. You say, "What about this and what about that?" It doesn't make any difference what comes your way! Paul called them "light afflictions" and until any of us are persecuted like Paul, we have no right calling them great afflictions. They are light. Somebody looks at us in the wrong way and we think we are going through great afflictions. These things that come our way are used by God to press us into the image of His dear Son. That is like pressing an elephant into a water bottle—there is a whole lot of flesh! Through every affliction we are going to see what truly is in our flesh, and then we can die to that area of our flesh. In everything give thanks, for this is the will of God concerning you. Things happen in our lives to bring us closer to God himself if only we will humble ourselves under His mighty hand.

It is when the Kingdom comes into our lives that we can understand how Paul could walk away from his life and become wholly obedient unto the leadership of the Holy Spirit. How he used his tent-making abilities to further the Kingdom. How he used what he had for the gospel. How he could rejoice in the Lord always—even when he did not understand what was happening in his life—by trusting that the Lord was working His will in his life and that Paul was being molded into the vessel God wanted him to be in eternity. Unfortunately, most people today are trying to use God for the things they want now. You will soon find out that you won't be able to go out and start a new church or ministry and make $1000 a week to start. It just won't happen. You are going to have to come to the place that your home, your car and your material possessions mean nothing to you, and they may be the instruments God wants to use for His purpose. In our lives, we held everything out to God so that our possessions were always for sale if that was the way God wanted to bring in money. Possessions can always be replaced; we did not value our things so much that we couldn't give them up. God became number one in our lives and then our family became second. Remember, the rich young ruler was told, "Sell what you have and give it to the poor and follow me." Possessions are no longer the treasures that you seek, only the opportunity to share God's good news to others, bringing to them the message of love, acceptance and forgiveness. Many of us have used things for our identification. We want to be important and think if we have the right home or car, we have 'made it'. But, we will only be important when we have crucified our flesh, and it is no longer us that are living, but Christ in us! Your treasure is above, you live for eternity and the urgency of the times causes you to press on to know the Lord.

When we begin to understand the purpose of our lives and who God has made us to be, we will discover that God has blessed us beyond what we can ask, hope or think. There is a big difference between your material things possessing you and you possessing them. The possessions are just a vehicle on this earth, and they are just temporary. Who God is looking for is faith-filled people who understand the concept of Kingdom living, are going about doing good and healing all who are oppressed by the devil because God is with them.

CHAPTER 11

THE SUMMATION

In hopes of grasping the entirety of the truths of God's Kingdom, mankind will fall far short. But, as we turn our lives over to Him, day-by-day, we will begin to see the Word of God fulfilled in our own lives. It is my hope that I can share with you through God's Word the truthfulness and integrity of His Word, how He truly has come to give us His kind of life and prosperity, that all things are truly working for our good, and that our time on earth is our training for our time to rule and reign with Him forever. I also want to share that our time on earth is the time we lay up treasure in heaven and how much we need to have an eternal vision so that we "don't sacrifice what we want most for what we want now." This time on earth is only a temporary life, so seek the eternal promises of God and live for heaven's sake!

THE LOSS OF RELATIONSHIP

In the Old Testament we discover a central theme: the establishment of the people of God and their expectation of His coming kingdom. We find that Adam and Eve sacrificed what they wanted most for that which they wanted now in the Garden of Eden by disobeying God's command not to eat of the fruit (Genesis 3:6). Mankind suffered spiritual death and loss of dominion, authority and humility in the earth.

The other sad thing that happened was found in Genesis 3:7, *"The eyes of them both were opened and they knew that they were naked."* Genesis 2:25 states, *"And they were both naked, the man and his wife, and were not ashamed."* What happened between Genesis 2:25 and Genesis 3:7? In Genesis 2:25, Adam and Eve were "God-conscience," but what died in Genesis 3:7 when they took of the fruit of the tree God had forbidden in Genesis 2:17? *"But of the tree of the knowledge of good and evil, thou shalt not eat of it; for in the day that thou eatest thereof thou shalt surely die."* They died spiritually; they no longer had an inner witness to God, and self-consciousness was born. Humility was lost and pride was born! At this point, man began his search for purpose and needed a savior to restore his relationship with God. All of mankind needed to be born again. Man had lost relationship with God, and God now began His restoration process.

Again this central theme in the Old Testament is the establishment of the people of God and their expectation of His coming kingdom. We also can identify God's plan for a coming savior through Jesus who was 100% God and 100% man on earth, and in His manhood He was the only person to live a sinless life.

Exodus 19:5-6, *"Now therefore, if ye will obey my voice indeed, and keep my covenant, then ye shall be a peculiar treasure unto me above all people: for all the earth is mine: and ye shall be unto me a kingdom of priests, and an holy nation."* From the beginning of time it has been God's plan to establish His Kingdom in the hearts and minds of His people. In doing so, His theocracy would be established.

From the beginning of time Satan's desire has been to destroy the people of God and the Word of God. He has even used the office of priest or pastor to lead and teach people, which has caused people to expect leadership to know the Word without having to know the Word themselves. This brought about a weak and defeated people lead by misguided leadership into the furnaces of destruction.

Genesis 1:26, *"And God said, Let us make man in our image, after our likeness: and let them have dominion over the fish of the sea, and over the fowl of the air, and over the cattle, and over all the earth, and over every creeping thing that creepeth upon the earth."* Genesis 3:1-5, *"Now the serpent was more subtle than any beast of the field which the LORD God had made. And he said unto the woman, Yea, hath God said, Ye shall not eat of every tree of the garden? And the woman said unto the serpent, We may eat of the fruit of the trees of the garden: But of the fruit of the tree which is in the midst of the garden, God hath said, Ye shall not eat of it, neither shall ye touch it, lest ye die. And the serpent said unto the woman, Ye shall not surely die: For God doth know that in the day ye eat thereof, then your eyes shall be opened, and ye shall be as gods, knowing good and evil"*—with the fall, man lost God-consciousness and self-consciousness was born—*"you shall surely die."*

Relationship and dominion were lost by mankind along with humility. With humility lost we find pride was born.

THE PROMISED SAVIOUR

God's Word clearly shows us His plan to restore our lost relationship through the promise of a Savior. These Scriptures underscore His promise.

Micah 5:2, *"But thou, Bethlehem Ephratah, though thou be little among the thousands of Judah, yet out of thee shall he come forth unto me that is to be ruler in Israel; whose goings forth have been from of old, from everlasting."*

Isaiah 7:14, *"Therefore the Lord himself shall give you a sign; Behold, a virgin shall conceive, and bear a son, and shall call his name Immanuel."*

Galatians 4:4, *"But when the fullness of the time was come, God sent forth his Son, made of a woman, made under the law."*

Isaiah 61:1-2, *"The Spirit of the Lord GOD is upon me; because the LORD hath anointed me to preach good tidings unto the meek; he hath sent me to bind up the brokenhearted, to proclaim liberty to the captives, and the opening of the prison to them that are bound; To proclaim the acceptable* year of the LORD, and the day of vengeance of our God; to comfort all that mourn."

Luke 4:16-21, "And he came to Nazareth, where he had been brought up: and, as his custom was, he went into the synagogue on the sabbath day, and stood up for to read. And there was delivered unto him the book of the prophet Esaias. And when he had opened the book, he found the place where it was written, The Spirit of the Lord is upon me, because he hath anointed me to preach the gospel to the poor; he hath sent me to heal the brokenhearted, to preach deliverance to the captives, and recovering of sight to the blind, to set at liberty them that are bruised, To preach the acceptable year of the Lord. And he closed the book, and he gave it again to the minister, and sat down. And the eyes of all them that were in the synagogue were fastened on him. And he began to say unto them, This day is this scripture fulfilled in your ears."

1 Timothy 3:16, "And without controversy great is the mystery of godliness: God was manifest in the flesh, justified in the Spirit, seen of angels, preached unto the Gentiles, believed on in the world, received up into glory."

Isaiah 9:6, "For unto us a child is born, unto us a son is given: and the government shall be upon his shoulder: and his name shall be called Wonderful, Counsellor, The mighty God, The everlasting Father, The Prince of Peace."

Philippians 2:5-6, "Let this mind be in you, which was also in Christ Jesus: Who, being in the form of God, thought it not robbery to be equal with God."

John 1:14, *"And the Word was made flesh and dwelt among us, (and we beheld his glory, the glory as of the only begotten of the Father,) full of grace and truth."* God in the flesh.

Matthew 1:18, 20, *"Now the birth of Jesus Christ was on this wise: When as his mother Mary was espoused to Joseph, before they came together, she was found with child of the Holy Ghost. But while he thought on these things, behold, the angel of the Lord appeared unto him in a dream, saying, Joseph, thou son of David, fear not to take unto thee Mary thy wife: for that which is conceived in her is of the Holy Ghost."* Luke 1:35, *"And the angel answered and said unto her, The Holy Ghost shall come upon thee, and the power of the Highest shall overshadow thee: therefore also that holy thing which shall be born of thee shall be called the Son of God."* Jesus Christ was conceived by God the Holy Spirit in the Virgin Mary's inner being. We call Him the Son of God because God the Holy Spirit conceived Him.

Hebrews 2:14-16, *"Forasmuch then as the children are partakers of flesh and blood, he also himself likewise took part of the same; that through death he might destroy him that had the power of death, that is, the devil; And deliver them who through fear of death were all their lifetime subject to bondage. For verily he took not on him the nature of angels; but he took on him the seed of Abraham."* God sent Jesus into the earth not as God only but as "The seed of Abraham." This is the covenant relationship that God made with Abraham in the Old Testament.

Galatians 3:3, *"Are ye so foolish? Having begun in the Spirit, are ye now made perfect by the flesh?"* Ephesians 2:8, *"For by grace are ye saved through faith; and that not of yourselves: it is the gift of God: not of works, lest any man should boast."* Jesus has come to replace the Old Testament covenant of works with the New Testament covenant of grace.

John 6:38, *"For I came down from heaven, not to do mine own will, but the will of him that sent me."* Jesus' victory came not from His soulish ability or strength but from His spiritual strength, which allowed Him to suffer humiliation and self-sacrifice upon the cross. He only did what the Father told Him to do.

Colossians 1:20, *"And, having made peace through the blood of his cross, by him to reconcile all things unto himself; by him, I say, whether they be things in earth, or things in heaven."* I John 1:7, *"But if we walk in the light, as he is in the light, we have fellowship one with another, and the blood of Jesus Christ his Son cleanseth us from all sin."* Revelation 1:5, *"And from Jesus Christ, who is the faithful witness, and the first begotten of the dead, and the prince of the kings of the earth. Unto him that loved us, and washed us from our sins in his own blood."* Revelation 5:9, *"And they sung a new song, saying, Thou art worthy to take the book, and to open the seals thereof: for thou wast slain, and hast redeemed us to God by thy blood out of every kindred, and tongue, and people, and nation."* Jesus provided His sinless blood on the cross so that mankind could be 100% forgiven of all sins.

Mark 1:14-15, *"After that John was put in prison, Jesus came into Galilee, preaching the gospel of the kingdom of God, and saying, The time is fulfilled, and the kingdom of God is at hand: repent ye, and believe the gospel."*

Isaiah 61:1-2, *"The Spirit of the Lord GOD is upon me; because the LORD hath anointed me to preach good tidings unto the meek; he hath sent me to bind up the brokenhearted, to proclaim liberty to the captives, and the opening of the prison to them that are bound; To proclaim the acceptable year of the LORD, and the day of vengeance of our God; to comfort all that mourn."*

Luke 17:21, *"Neither shall they say, Lo here! or, lo there! for, behold, the kingdom of God is within you."*

ENTRANCE INTO THE PROMISED LIFE

After the fall of mankind in the Garden of Eden, mankind needed a savior to restore us back to God our Creator. Jesus gave His life and His blood to cover our sins and restore us back to God. We then are saved by God's grace (His undeserved favor), through faith in Jesus Christ and His death, burial and resurrection. Salvation is a gift from God, not of our works or human effort or purpose. Salvation is not intellectual acceptance, but heartfelt repentance and victory.

God gave us His Word, the Bible, to help lead and guide us into His truth. Left alone without the Word, we live in darkness and ignorance to the plan of God, which only leads us further into confusion. Without meditating the Word, we are left without truth, and without truth we will have no peace.

Many today have chosen the wide road to destruction because they are too busy to attend unto the Word of God. We are "addicted to activity" and in our world today we don't "have time" to study the Word. But, without knowledge of the Word, we will not understand our purpose and just become people addicted to human activity as opposed to becoming "doers of the Word!" We find many misguided people today reflecting Old Testament legalism, the do's and don'ts, instead of New Testament love and grace. Love and grace will change the life of the powerless sinner into becoming a powerful over comer. Legalism leaves people in despair and without hope because they cannot change their lives simply by behavior modification in their own ability. It can only be changed by the power of the Holy Spirit.

1. Galatians 2:16, *"Knowing that a man is not justified by the works of the law, but by the faith of Jesus Christ, even we have believed in Jesus Christ, that we might be justified by the faith of Christ, and not by the works of the law: for by the works of the law shall no flesh be justified."*

2. Ephesians 2:8-9, *"For by grace are ye saved through faith; and that not of yourselves: it is the gift of God: Not of works, lest any man should boast."*

3. John 7:16-18, *"Jesus answered them, and said, My doctrine is not mine, but his that sent me. If any man will do his will, he shall know of the doctrine, whether*

it be of God, or whether I speak of myself. He that speaketh of himself seeketh his own glory: but he that seeketh his glory that sent him, the same is true, and no unrighteousness is in him."

4. John 3:16, "God so loved the world, that he gave his only begotten Son, that whosoever believeth in him should not perish, but have everlasting life."

5. Romans 10:9-10, "That if thou shalt confess with thy mouth the Lord Jesus, and shalt believe in thine heart that God hath raised him from the dead, thou shalt be saved. For with the heart man believeth unto righteousness; and with the mouth confession is made unto salvation."

6. Matthew 16:19, "And I will give unto thee the keys of the kingdom of heaven: and whatsoever thou shalt bind on earth shall be bound in heaven: and whatsoever thou shalt loose on earth shall be loosed in heaven." The keys of the Kingdom must be known and applied for us to see the blessings and power of the Kingdom.

7. Matthew 6: 33-34, "But seek ye first the kingdom of God, and his righteousness; and all these things shall be added unto you. Take therefore no thought for the morrow: for the morrow shall take thought for the things of itself. Sufficient unto the day is the evil thereof."

8. God's Kingdom transcends all earthly concerns and needs.

9. In God's Kingdom, every believer is called to be a priest and part of the priesthood. As we look into the Old Testament, we see that we as priests are called to be a blessing. Leviticus 9:23-24, *"And Moses and Aaron went into the tabernacle of the congregation, and came out, and blessed the people: and the glory of the LORD appeared unto all the people. And there came a fire out from before the LORD, and consumed upon the altar the burnt offering and the fat: which when all the people saw, they shouted, and fell on their faces."* We find in Numbers 6:27, *"So shall they put My name upon the people of Israel, and I will bless them."* Some denominations have set up men as "priests" to head the church and give the sacraments, but that is not what Jesus is saying. The priesthood is not just select men called by man, but all truly born-again Christians who have submitted themselves under the mighty hand of God and separated themselves from the darkness of the world.

In 1 Peter 2:9, all born-again believers are called to be a royal priesthood to bless and bring joy, and to walk as priests bringing forgiveness and reconciliation to the world through Jesus Christ. We have been called and chosen by God for the work of this priestly ministry to walk in love and bring good news to a condemned world.

The Lord has opened wide the gates of heaven and proclaimed unto us in Hebrews 10:19-22, *"Having therefore, brethren, boldness to enter into the holiest by the blood of Jesus, By a new and living way, which he hath consecrated for us, through the veil, that is to say, his flesh; And having an high priest over the house of God; Let us draw near with a true heart in full assurance of faith, having our hearts sprinkled from an evil conscience, and our bodies washed with pure water."* Let us walk in love and bring God's reconciliation and forgiveness to our world.

10. God's promise of a new life is found in 2 Corinthians 5:17, *"Therefore, if anyone is in Christ, he is a new creation; old things have passed away; behold, all things have become new."* Have you ever thought to yourself, "I wish I could start my life over?" Through Jesus Christ we can do exactly that. He forgives us for our past and makes us a brand new creation when we are "born again." Then according to Luke 14:33, *"So likewise, whosoever he be of you that forsaketh not all that he hath, he cannot be my disciple."* If we do not renounce all we have, we cannot be His disciple. This represents an absolute, complete surrender unto Him. The more we give to Him, the more we have of Him in our lives.

Romans 6:6 says, *"Knowing this, that our old man was crucified with Him, that the body of sin might be done away with, that we should no longer be slaves of sin."* When we are born again, God places who we were upon the cross with Jesus and the old man is crucified with Him. When this happens, the power of the Holy Spirit states in Galatians 4:6, *"And because you are sons, God has sent forth the Spirit of His son into your hearts, crying out, Abba Father!"* The Spirit is sent into our lives to give us a new nature and power over all the works of the enemy, setting us free from the addictive sinfulness of our past to be free to start over with the power of the Holy Spirit. Roman 6:12 then tells us, *"Therefore do not let sin reign in your mortal body, that you should obey it in its lusts."* If we look at Galatians 5:19-21 we find many of the works of the flesh listed, and we can then set our hearts to walk away from them and resist them in Jesus' name.

Galatians 2:20 states: *"I am crucified with Christ: nevertheless I live; yet not I, but Christ liveth in me: and the life which I now live in the flesh I live by the faith of the Son of God, who loved me, and gave himself for me."* Because of what Jesus has done for us, we have been forgiven and born again so we now can live our lives by the faith of the Son of God. Galatians 5:16 says, *"So I say, live by the spirit, and you will not gratify the desires of the sinful nature."* When we seek Jesus and His lordship, the sinful desires of the flesh can no longer control our lives because, *"Whom the Son sets free is free indeed."*

11. Acts 10:36-43 states very clearly in the New Testament that the Messiah has come in the person of Jesus of Nazareth! This same Jesus demonstrated to us the spirit-filled life that God Himself desires we walk in: healing the sick, raising the dead and walking in signs, wonders and miracles—actions only a miraculous

God in His power could manifest. Jesus didn't come as God on earth, but as the "Seed of Abraham" according to Hebrews 2:14-16, demonstrating through his humanity the power God has given to His covenant people. This is the same Jesus who died and rose again, and was lifted up into heaven according to the Word of God. This is Jesus who will also come and judge the quick and the dead.

12. Acts 13:12-16, *"Then the deputy, when he saw what was done, believed, being astonished at the doctrine of the Lord. Now when Paul and his company loosed from Paphos, they came to Perga in Pamphylia: and John departing from them returned to Jerusalem. But when they departed from Perga, they came to Antioch in Pisidia, and went into the synagogue on the Sabbath day, and sat down. And after the reading of the law and the prophets the rulers of the synagogue sent unto them, saying, Ye men and brethren, if ye have any word of exhortation for the people, say on. Then Paul stood up, and beckoning with his hand said, Men of Israel, and ye that fear God, give audience."*

13. Luke 12:3, *"Therefore whatsoever ye have spoken in darkness shall be heard in the light; and that which ye have spoken in the ear in closets shall be proclaimed upon the housetops."*

14. Revelation 3:20, *"Behold, I stand at the door, and knock: if any man hear my voice, and open the door, I will come in to him, and will sup with him, and he with me."*

15. Galatians 2:20, *"I am crucified with Christ: nevertheless I live; yet not I, but Christ liveth in me: and the life which I now live in the flesh I live by the faith of the Son of God, who loved me, and gave himself for me."*

16. 2 Corinthians 5:17, *"Therefore if any man be in Christ, he is a new creature: old things are passed away; behold all things are become new."*

17. *"Thy kingdom come."*

THE PROMISED CHURCH

God promised a worldwide Church in which all the powers of hell would attempt to defeat, but would not prevail. He has given His people power over all the power of the enemy and allowed His dominion and authority to work through them. Many today have reached the point of spiritual blindness and hardness of hearts and have allowed lying spirits to alter the truth of God. Hearts have been led away from God and into idolatry and covetousness.

Popularity seems to grasp many leaders today; however, Jesus stated in John 15:17 that if the world loves you, you are not His. Jesus has called us to come out of the world and be conformed to His image, and deny ourselves and pick up our cross and follow Him. The crucified life is not a popular message in the church today; however, it remains the foundation of truth for our transformation into the body of Christ. Permissive Christians are seeking out permissive teachers to help justify their lives rather than accepting the message of crucifixion and bringing resurrection into their lives. Without the crucifixion of our lives we will never see the resurrection of "Christ in us the hope of glory."

This church is not a denomination or a building, but a group of people who have experienced the saving power of Jesus Christ in their lives. The Kingdom is made up of people who have declared the Lordship of Jesus over their lives. And when Jesus is Lord over their lives He has given them power over all the power of the enemy. By faith in His name, the name of Jesus, these can take back dominion and authority over their lives and His world. They are following in His footsteps of radical obedience, which no man except Jesus has obtained, and are "pressing on to the mark the high calling of the Lord." Sin and carnality must be removed from us as individuals for the life of God to truly shine through us. Many today are looking only to use the church for their own glory and that is why many are failing. Self-indulgence seems to me to be the sin of the church today. The Kingdom is people who are demonstrating to the world the righteousness of God through the power of the Holy Spirit.

Mark 1:15, "And saying, The time is fulfilled, and the kingdom of God is at hand: repent ye, and believe the gospel."

Luke 10:23-24, "And he turned him unto his disciples, and said privately, Blessed are the eyes which see the things that ye see: For I tell you, that many prophets and kings have desired to see those things which ye see, and have not seen them; and to hear those things which ye hear, and have not heard them."

214

1 Peter 2:9-10, *"But ye are a chosen generation, a royal priesthood, an holy nation, a peculiar people; that ye should show forth the praises of him who hath called you out of darkness into his marvelous light: Which in time past were not a people, but are now the people of God: which had not obtained mercy, but now have obtained mercy."*

Revelation 1:6, *"And hath made us kings and priests unto God and his Father; to him be glory and dominion forever and ever. Amen."*

Revelation 5:10, *"And hast made us unto our God kings and priests: and we shall reign on the earth."*

1 Corinthians 12:27, *"Now ye are the body of Christ, and members in particular."* In Ephesians 1:22-23 God tells us what His body is: *"And He put all things under His feet, and gave Him to be head over all things to the church, which is His body, the fullness of Him who fills all in all."* The body of Christ is the same as the church. God uses both terms to identify those that have believed upon the Lord Jesus Christ as their savior. These are those who have been separated by God from the world into His Kingdom of God (Colossians 1:13).

In I Corinthians 6:19-20, our body is called, *"the temple of the Holy Spirit, which is in you, which you have from God, and ye are not your own."* We are no longer our own, our lives are no longer our own to do with what we please, but they now belong to God and are to be used for His purposes. Verse 20 says, *"For ye are bought with a price: therefore glorify God in your body, and in your spirit, which are God's."* We belong to God and He wants to show Himself strong in our lives for

215

the purposes each and every one of us has been called to.

There is restlessness in the body of Christ today, and many are fleeing the denominations for the desire to be what Christ has called them to be—the body of Christ. People are tired of just helping around the church and are breaking out, seeking a personal relationship with Christ, desiring the leadership of the Holy Spirit and are truly reflecting Jesus. They are realizing the different gifting of each other and the need for those gifting and uniquenesses to be utilized in the body of Christ. These are the true worshippers of God, those who have a heart and love for Him and a sincere heart to follow Him. The man-made barriers created by the denominations are being broken down, and Christians are beginning to walk in love with each other, demonstrating the universal church of Jesus. It is not what denomination you belong to, but rather whether you are truly born again and have a personal relationship with the King of Kings and Lord of Lords.

Matthew 16:15-19, *"He saith unto them, But whom say ye that I am? And Simon Peter answered and said, Thou art the Christ, the Son of the living God. And Jesus answered and said unto him, Blessed art thou, Simon Barjona: for flesh and blood hath not revealed it unto thee, but my Father which is in heaven. And I say also unto thee, That thou art Peter, and upon this rock I will build my church; and the gates of hell shall not prevail against it. And I will give unto thee the keys of the kingdom of heaven: and whatsoever thou shalt bind on earth shall be bound in heaven: and whatsoever thou shalt loose on earth shall be loosed in heaven."*

The rock being identified as the revelation that Jesus is God.

Christ didn't call us to a place of strength and power in the flesh, rather He called us to a place of being the least of all and becoming the servant of others.

THE PROMISED PEOPLE

The promised people are those who have willingly laid down their lives and have chosen to follow Him. They have realized that for Jesus to increase they must decrease. They have given their lives, wills and futures to the Lord of Lords and King of Kings and are letting His marvelous light (1 Peter 2:9) shine through them.

1. Galatians 6 tells us God's purpose in coming was also to give His people power over the flesh by giving us the power of the Holy Spirit to return us to a moral and ethical position in His body.

2. 1 Corinthians 6:9-11, *"Know ye not that the unrighteous shall not inherit the kingdom of God? Be not deceived: neither fornicators, nor idolaters, nor adulterers, nor effeminate, nor abusers of themselves with mankind, Nor thieves, nor covetous, nor drunkards, nor revilers, nor extortioners, shall inherit the kingdom of God. And such were some of you: but ye are washed, but ye are sanctified, but ye are justified in the name of the Lord Jesus, and by the Spirit of our God."*

3. Philippians 3:20-21, *"For our conversation is in heaven; from whence also we look for the Saviour, the Lord Jesus Christ: Who shall change our vile body, that it may be fashioned like unto his glorious body, according to the working whereby he is able even to subdue all things unto himself."*

4. John 18:36, *"Jesus answered, My kingdom is not of this world: if my kingdom were of this world, then would my servants fight, that I should not be delivered to the Jews: but now is my kingdom not from hence."*

   John 17:16, *"They are not of the world, even as I am not of the world."*

5. Matthew 25:31-46, *"When the Son of man shall come in his glory, and all the holy angels with him, then shall he sit upon the throne of his glory: And before him shall be gathered all nations: and he shall separate them one from another, as a shepherd divideth his sheep from the goats: And he shall set the sheep on his right hand, but the goats on the left. Then shall the King say unto them on his right hand, Come, ye blessed of my Father, inherit the kingdom prepared for you from the foundation of the world: For I was an hungered, and ye gave me meat: I was thirsty, and ye gave me drink: I was a stranger, and ye took me in: Naked, and ye clothed me: I was sick, and ye visited me: I was in prison, and ye came unto me. Then shall the righteous answer him, saying, Lord, when saw we thee an hungered, and fed thee? or thirsty, and gave*

*thee drink? When saw we thee a stranger, and took
thee in? or naked, and clothed thee? Or when saw we
thee sick, or in prison, and came unto thee? And the
King shall answer and say unto them, Verily I say unto
you, Inasmuch as ye have done it unto one of the least
of these my brethren, ye have done it unto me. Then
shall he say also unto them on the left hand, Depart
from me, ye cursed, into everlasting fire, prepared for
the devil and his angels: For I was an hungered, and
ye gave me no meat: I was thirsty, and ye gave me no
drink: I was a stranger, and ye took me not in: naked,
and ye clothed me not: sick, and in prison, and ye
visited me not. Then shall they also answer him, saying, Lord, when saw we thee an hungered, or athirst,
or a stranger, or naked, or sick, or in prison, and did
not minister unto thee? Then shall he answer them,
saying, Verily I say unto you, Inasmuch as ye did it not
to one of the least of these, ye did it not to me. And
these shall go away into everlasting punishment: but
the righteous into life eternal."*

6. Colossians 3:9-10, *"Lie not one to another, seeing that
ye have put off the old man with his deeds; And have
put on the new man, which is renewed in knowledge
after the image of him that created him."*

7. Hebrews 11:6, *"But without faith it is impossible to
please him: for he that cometh to God must believe
that he is, and that he is a rewarder of them that
diligently seek him."*

8. John 12:24-26, *"Verily, verily, I say unto you, Except a corn of wheat fall into the ground and die, it abideth alone: but if it die, it bringeth forth much fruit. He that loveth his life shall lose it; and he that hateth his life in this world shall keep it unto life eternal. If any man serve me, let him follow me; and where I am, there shall also my servant be: if any man serve me, him will my Father honour."*

9. Mark 8:34-38, *"And when he had called the people unto him with his disciples also, he said unto them, Whosoever will come after me, let him deny himself, and take up his cross, and follow me. For whosoever will save his life shall lose it; but whosoever shall lose his life for my sake and the gospel's, the same shall save it. For what shall it profit a man, if he shall gain the whole world, and lose his own soul? Or what shall a man give in exchange for his soul? Whosoever therefore shall be ashamed of me and of my words in this adulterous and sinful generation; of him also shall the Son of man be ashamed, when he cometh in the glory of his Father with the holy angels."*

THE PROMISED PROVISION

In Matthew 6:19-34, God has shown us a pattern for receiving His provision. As we seek His Kingdom as opposed to our own, "the kingdom of self," we begin to see His provision manifested in our lives. God has called us to His purpose, and we become His ambassadors on earth. In exchange for us yielding our lives and our purposes, He gives us the provision to fulfill His will through our lives on earth. Let God's own Word speak to you.

1. Matthew 6:33-34, *"But seek ye first the kingdom of God, and his righteousness; and all these things shall be added unto you. Take therefore no thought for the morrow: for the morrow shall take thought for the things of itself. Sufficient unto the day is the evil thereof."*

2. Philippians 4:19, *"But my God shall supply all your need according to his riches in glory by Christ Jesus."*

3. Psalms 37:25-26, *"I have been young, and now am old; yet have I not seen the righteous forsaken, nor his seed begging bread. He is ever merciful, and lendeth; and his seed is blessed."*

4. Luke 6:38, *"Give, and it shall be given unto you; good measure, pressed down, and shaken together, and running over, shall men give into your bosom. For with the same measure that ye mete withal it shall be measured to you again."*

5. Luke 18:22, *"Now when Jesus heard these things, he said unto him, Yet lackest thou one thing: sell all that thou hast, and distribute unto the poor, and thou shalt have treasure in heaven: and come, follow me."*

6. It is in truly loving others as we love ourselves that we are able to give in a godly way and sow into prosperous fields of God's blessings.

THE PROMISED PURPOSE

What then is God's purpose for my life? This we find throughout the Bible.

1. Matthew 28:19-20, *"Go ye therefore, and teach all nations, baptizing them in the name of the Father, and of the Son, and of the Holy Ghost: Teaching them to observe all things whatsoever I have commanded you: and, lo, I am with you always, even unto the end of the world. Amen."*

2. Mark 9:35, *"And he sat down, and called the twelve, and saith unto them, If any man desire to be first, the same shall be last of all, and servant of all."*

3. John 13:14-17, *"If I then, your Lord and Master, have washed your feet; ye also ought to wash one another's feet. For I have given you an example, that ye should do as I have done to you. Verily, verily, I say unto you, The servant is not greater than his lord; neither he that is sent greater than he that sent him. If ye know these things, happy are ye if ye do them."*

4. Matthew 11:28-30, *"Come unto me, all ye that labour and are heavy laden, and I will give you rest. Take my yoke upon you, and learn of me; for I am meek and lowly in heart: and ye shall find rest unto your souls. For my yoke is easy, and my burden is light."*

5. John 17:18-19, 23, *"As thou hast sent me into the world, even so have I also sent them into the world. And for their sakes I sanctify myself, that they also might be sanctified through the truth. I in them, and thou in me, that they may be made perfect in one; and that the world may know that thou hast sent me, and hast loved them, as thou hast loved me."*

6. 11 Corinthians 4:11, *"For we which live are always delivered unto death for Jesus' sake, that the life also of Jesus might be made manifest in our mortal flesh."*

7. Psalms 8:4-6, *"What is man, that thou art mindful of him? And the son of man, that thou visitest him? For thou hast made him a little lower than the angels, and hast crowned him with glory and honour. Thou madest him to have dominion over the works of thy hands; thou hast put all things under his feet."*

THE PROMISED FUTURE

Have you ever wondered what happens after you die? Before I became a Christian I did, and even as a young Christian I did, but the Word has set me free and given me understanding about our future.

Jesus Christ spoke a great deal about eternity. He told us He came to earth from a place called heaven, and that after He was crucified, died and buried, He would return to that great place. Without going into great detail, I will share the

Word and what it says about our future. We will see heaven is a place where God and His followers live, and it will come down to earth and reside with mankind in the end.

Because I am writing to Christian people, I will not be going into great detail about hell—a real and a horrible place for those who have rejected God. If you have gotten this far in the book and are truly hungry for the things of God, you can seek the Word about the existence of hell. As you study about it, your purpose in the earth will be brought to your understanding. Salvation is not just about escaping hell; it is truly about a relationship with our heavenly Father.

This world is temporal, but we are headed to our promised future, to another place when we die, and that place is called heaven. We will reside there until the end times, and we will then come back to this place called earth. There is going to be the last Great War on earth between God and His people, and Satan and the ungodly. This world will then be blown up and consumed by fire (2 Peter 3:10). God will build a new earth and a new heaven right here on earth in the area where Jerusalem, Israel, exists. He will build the new Jerusalem, the seat of His government. In this new earth, Satan will no longer exist as he will have been thrown in the Lake of Fire. In this new world, there will no longer be sickness and disease, no more trials and temptations, no more struggles. Instead, there will be continual joy and peace, and God's Kingdom in its fullness will truly have become. Righteousness, which is us being in right standing with God, will evoke into our lives right doing and bring forth God's peace into our lives. When God's peace is in our hearts it invokes the joy of the Lord, which according to the Word of God, is our strength (Romans 14:17). Also Nehemiah 8:10 states, "For the joy of the Lord is your strength." What a great and wonderful future we have as believers!

Revelation 21: 1-8, *"And I saw a new heaven and a new earth: for the first heaven and the first earth were passed away; and there was no more sea. And I John saw the holy city, new Jerusalem, coming down from God out of heaven, prepared as a bride adorned for her husband. And I heard a great voice out of heaven saying, Behold, the tabernacle of God is with men, and he will dwell with them, and they shall be his people, and God himself shall be with them, and be their God. And God shall wipe away all tears from their eyes; and there shall be no more death, neither sorrow, nor crying, neither shall there be any more pain: for the former things are passed away. And he that sat upon the throne said, Behold, I make all things new. And he said unto me, Write: for these words are true and faithful. And he said unto me, It is done. I am Alpha and Omega, the beginning and the end. I will give unto him that is athirst of the fountain of the water of life freely. He that overcometh shall inherit all things; and I will be his God, and he shall be my son. But the fearful, and unbelieving, and the abominable, and murderers, and whoremongers, and sorcerers, and idolaters, and all liars, shall have their part in the lake which burneth with fire and brimstone: which is the second death."*

Revelation 22:6-21, *"And he said unto me, These sayings are faithful and true: and the Lord God of the holy prophets sent his angel to show unto his servants the things which must shortly be done. Behold, I come quickly: blessed is he that* keepeth the sayings of the prophecy of this book. And I John saw these things, and heard them. And when I had heard and seen, I fell down to worship before the feet of the angel which showed me these things. Then saith he unto me, See thou do it not: for I am thy fellow servant, and of thy brethren the prophets, and of them which keep the sayings of this book: worship God. And he saith unto me, Seal not the sayings of the prophecy of this book: for the time is at hand. He that is unjust, let him be unjust still: and he which is filthy, let him be filthy still: and he that is righteous, let him be righteous still: and he that is holy, let him be holy still. And, behold, I come quickly; and my reward is with me, to give every man according as his work shall be. I am Alpha and Omega, the beginning and the end, the first and the last. Blessed are they that do his commandments that they may have right to the tree of life, and may enter in through the gates into the city. For without are dogs, and sorcerers, and whoremongers, and murderers, and idolaters, and whosoever loveth and maketh a lie. I Jesus have sent mine angel to testify unto you these things in the churches. I am the root and the offspring of David, and the bright and morning star. And the Spirit and the bride say, Come. And let him that heareth say, Come. And let him that is athirst come. And whosoever will, let him take the water of life freely. For I testify unto every man that heareth the words of the prophecy of this book, If any man shall add unto these things, God shall add unto him the plagues that are written in this book: And if any man shall take away from the words of the book of this prophecy, God shall take away his part out of the book of life, and out of the holy city, and from the things which are written in this book. He which testifieth these things *saith, Surely I come quickly. Amen. Even so, come, Lord Jesus. The grace of our Lord Jesus Christ be with you all. Amen."*

May the Lord of harvest bless us in all spiritual wisdom and understanding.